FRESH MOROCCAN

NADA SALEH

hamlyn

NOTE

Both metric and imperial measurements have been given in all recipes. Use one set of measurements only and not a mixture of both.

Standard level spoon measurements are used in all recipes.
1 tablespoon = one 15 ml spoon
1 teaspoon = one 5 ml spoon

The Department of Health advises that eggs should not be consumed raw. This book contains dishes made with raw or lightly cooked eggs. It is prudent for vulnerable people such as pregnant and nursing mothers, invalids, the elderly, babies and young children to avoid uncooked or lightly cooked dishes made with eggs. Once prepared, these dishes should be kept refrigerated and used promptly.

This book includes dishes made with nuts and nut derivatives. It is advisable for those with known allergic reactions to nuts and nut derivatives and those who may be potentially vulnerable to these allergies, such as pregnant and nursing mothers, invalids, the elderly, babies and children to avoid dishes made with nuts and nut oils. It is also prudent to check the labels of pre-prepared ingredients for the possible inclusion of nut derivatives.

Ovens should be preheated to the specified temperature – if using a fan-assisted oven, follow the manufacturer's instructions for adjusting the time and the temperature.

An Hachette Livre UK Company
www.hachettelivre.co.uk

First published in Great Britain in 2007 by
Hamlyn, a division of Octopus Publishing Group Ltd
2–4 Heron Quays, London E14 4JP
www.octopusbooks.co.uk

Copyright © Octopus Publishing Group Ltd 2007

The material in this book was previously published in *Fresh Moroccan*

ISBN: 978-0-600-61687-0

A CIP catalogue record for this book is available from the British Library

Printed and bound in China

10 9 8 7 6 5 4 3 2

CONTENTS

INTRODUCTION

My journey around Morocco started in the ancient city of Marrakech, founded in 1062 and an important crossroads for caravans as well as a meeting place for traders. At the famous Jemaa el-Fna market, where clouds of smoke rose from restaurant stalls busy grilling *kefta* and *merguez*, I saw storytellers, a snake charmer, a woman fortune-teller and young men – made-up and dressed in women's clothing – belly dancing. A visit to the souk, a network of alleyways, revealed many souks within souks, but the one that fascinated me most of all sold fruits, vegetables, pyramids of colourful spices, buckets of purple, green and black olives, and lemon and pepper confits. I saw heaps of pomegranates, introduced by the Phoenicians, who came to Morocco during their voyages in the 4th and 5th centuries BC, and who also brought the olive tree. Oranges, lemons, figs, dates, aubergines, artichokes, apricots, saffron and much more were later introduced by the Arabs.

To the west of Marrakech lies Essaouira, a fortified town on the Atlantic coast. Here I sampled delicious specialities such as Fish Tagine with Couscous, cooked with onions and raisins *(see page 174)* and Sardines in Aromatic Herbs – balls of minced sardine in tomato sauce *(see page 166)*. Further down the coast is Agadir, famous for its sardine fisheries, while inland to the east is the village of Sidi al Mukhtar, which produces cumin, much used in Moroccan cuisine, and Tarazout, where bananas are grown.

In the Atlas mountains the people of a Berber village greeted me and with great generosity prepared the specialities of the region, such as *Urkimen* (couscous of barley semolina, *see page 190), Amlou (see page 12)* and many others, to which each family contributed. One brought the onions, another the corn, some the almonds and the honey, and so on.

Among the rocks and hills of the Atlas mountains, cactuses abound, and the prickly pear fruit (barbary fig) can be found. The thorns are removed using palm leaves, then the skin is peeled and the fruit is dried in the sun to use in winter in couscous in some regions. In summer when the prickly pear is ripe, sellers slice open the fruit, which are orange in colour and very tasty. The mountain evenings are cool, and I welcomed the nourishing Berber tagines of meat, carrots, potatoes, peas and olives, such as the one I enjoyed at Tafraout. My first trip to Morocco years ago was to Fez, one of the holiest places in Morocco. I was then, as I still am today, overwhelmed by its mysterious and magical appeal. The market, a labyrinth of narrow alleyways, is a magnet to shoppers and a feast for the senses. Aromas of wild herbs and spices mingle with street food, while the sight of fruit and vegetables makes you dream of the filo pie B'steeya with Chicken *(see page 108)*, for which Fez is famous, delicious tagines such as *Maqfoul*, Lamb with Tomatoes and Onions *(see page 148)*, and the fig and walnut dishes of the south, or the apricot and almond dishes of the north of the country.

Many dynasties have ruled Morocco causing many diverse influences to be reflected in her culture and way of life. Moroccan cuisine seems to be distinct from that of the Middle Eastern and the other North African cuisines, as if to make a statement of independence and pride. Independence, for the Ottomans stopped their expansion more or less on the Kingdom's borders, and pride, for Morocco was the springboard and the main source of manpower for the invasion and occupation of Spain from the 8th century AD onwards. A prestigious past and a population of different cultures, the Berbers, Arabs and Jews have left their mark on the present-day cuisine. Many dishes that appear in ancient Arab literature are evidence of this influence.

Sharing regular meals is an important factor in the life of Moroccans and home cooking is a natural part of everyday life – it's a joy for everyone and brings the family together. Throughout this book you will find wholesome recipes that promote health and longevity. They are low in fat and in salt and are therefore a good choice for those who wish to lose excess weight.

NADA SALEH

HEALTHY EATING

We live at a time when there is much controversy about what we eat. One day we are told how beneficial a foodstuff is, while the next we are advised to avoid it. Should we use butter or is it high in saturated fats? Would it be better to follow the high-protein Atkins diet or should we become vegetarians? How can we tell what is best and how can we look after our health?

A BALANCED DIET

In my early teens my first concern was to stay slim at any cost. I could have avoided my repeated diets and resulting weight gain if I had just eaten the nutritious home-cooked meals that my mother provided. I deprived myself of the foods and fats essential for building the immune system and providing the vital fuel for achieving high levels of mental and emotional balance. I took this risk until I learnt how important these foods are for our physical as well as our mental wellbeing. Now my eating plan is backed by scientific research, logic, common sense and the wisdom of our forebears.

Cooking wholesome dishes preserves one's health and vitality, and they don't necessarily require expensive ingredients. Stock up with beans, chickpeas, lentils, peas, couscous, rice, spices, olive oil, nuts and seeds and so on – all valuable sources of vegetable protein, vitamins and minerals. Serve them with fresh vegetables to produce delicious meals for your family and friends. With home cooking, you know what's on your plate since you're in control of the quality and quantity of the ingredients.

SWEET TREATS

Life can have cruel moments and sometimes we find ourselves reaching for fatty and sugary foods that provide temporary comfort. Instead, make snacks such as briouats, milk puddings, soups and salads so that when you open the refrigerator you will always find something nourishing and satisfying to eat.

Having treats for dessert is fine, but rather than indulging in high-fat, high-sugar sweets, prepare instead dishes such as Rice Pudding with Almonds *(see page 236)* or Dried Fruit Salad *(see page 242)*. By eating healthily, you can relax after a meal without feeling guilty about having eaten unnecessary calories. Or, if you wish to cut out desserts but still want to satisfy a sweet tooth, try tagines such as Lamb Tagine with Prunes and Apricots *(see page 120)* and Chicken, Chickpeas and Raisins *(see page 102)*.

REDUCING FAT IN YOUR DIET

Nonetheless, fats are warming and good sources of energy; they cushion and protect body organs, keep brain and body cells healthy, calm the nerves and are necessary for the assimilation of the fat-soluble vitamins A, D, E and K. There are three types of fats: saturated fatty acids, found in meat, cheese, butter, egg yolk, cream and palm oil; monounsaturated fatty acids, found in olive and groundnut oils, avocados and olives; and polyunsaturated fatty acids, including the essential oils omega-3 and omega-6 found in corn, argan, soya bean, safflower and sunflower oils, sesame seeds, walnuts and oily fish.

A lifetime commitment to good eating habits is vital for building immunity and mental alertness. Many studies of the diets of Mediterranean countries show that those who follow these diets have a low percentage of heart problems, high blood pressure, cancers and also memory loss. These findings show that you should eat a varied diet and cut back on saturated fats, as these are increasingly linked to cardiovascular problems, many cancers, obesity, high levels of bad cholesterol (LDL) and much more.

I have therefore sought out cuisines with dishes high in nutritional value but low in saturated fats such as butter. Moroccan food fits these criteria. It delivers a substantial variety of dishes with intriguing mixtures of ingredients, with plenty of flavour and an abundance of nutrients to satisfy bodily needs. For example, the famous B'steeya *(see page 108)* is a rich mixture of chicken or pigeon, herbs, spices, eggs and almonds enveloped in layers of *warka* (filo pastry). Cutting down on the butter used in the pastry makes it easier to digest.

Complex carbohydrate dishes are another example. They are an excellent source of vegetable protein, protect the body and help counteract insomnia and stress. They include dishes such as Barley Semolina Soup *(see page 34)*. Another warming soup is *Harira (see page 32)*; during the month of Ramadan, the fast is broken with *Harira*

served with dates and briouats, supplying the body with vital protein, vitamins, minerals and energy. Fish dishes are excellent, too – Prawns M'chermel in Tomato Sauce *(see page 170)* and sardines are a good source of omega-3 fatty acids, an essential oil that feeds brain cells, reduces bad cholesterol (LDL) and is anti-ageing.

Moroccan food has many health-giving properties. For instance, onions and garlic help prevent high blood pressure. Chicken and almonds are a good source of protein and of tryptophan, a natural remedy for insomnia. Herbs such as coriander, parsley, mint and thyme help to keep the circulation flowing, detoxify the body and aid digestion.

PROMOTING GOOD HEALTH

Experiment with healthy ingredients, remembering at all times that the key to good health is balance, moderation and positive thinking combined with a sensible exercise and meditation routine. Too much of anything can have a detrimental effect on one's health.

EQUIPMENT

The utensils and equipment used in the Moroccan kitchen do not differ much from those in European ones, except for the couscoussière.

ELECTRIC FOOD PROCESSOR, BLENDER OR MIXER to chop, mince and purée vegetables, grains and pulses, fish, meat or chicken.

PANS A selection of heavy-based frying pans, casseroles and nonstick pans in different sizes. Do not use aluminium pans – the metal leaches into the food.

COUSCOUSSIERE – a double pan. Stews and flavoured stocks are cooked in the lower part, while the perforated upper part is used to steam couscous, vegetables, fish and meat.

MORTAR AND PESTLE These are useful for creaming garlic or herbs and grinding spices and mastic (gum arabic). I like wooden ones as the slightly rough interior surface aids the creaming or crushing. Always sprinkle a little salt over garlic and herbs, and sugar over mastic, before crushing; pound gently and rub against the mortar base.

SIEVES AND STRAINERS in different sizes are useful for skimming, draining and straining.

WOODEN SPOONS in various sizes. These are strong, practical, lightweight and heat-resistant.

KNIVES One good knife to chop herbs, vegetables and fruits and another for meat, fish and chicken. Use a sharpening steel to keep knives sharp.

ADDITIONAL EQUIPMENT Spatulas, scissors, scales, measuring jugs and spoons, and glass food containers are always useful.

HOW TO PREPARE COUSCOUS

To cook couscous the traditional way (using uncooked couscous, not the precooked variety that is commonly sold), the grains are rinsed and drained, then spread over a large wooden tray or shallow pan and aerated, using the fingers in a circular movement. They are then left for 15–30 minutes until the water is fully absorbed and the grains are relatively dry. Then the grains are gently rubbed between the palms to break down any lumps. Next, they are transferred to the perforated top section

of the couscoussière, placed over the lower part, which is filled two-thirds full with boiling water or a stew and left to steam. While steaming the grains, do not cover them with a lid, otherwise they will become soggy. The steam from the lower part enters through the holes to cook the grains.

When steam escapes through the grains, remove and spread them over the tray or pan. Moisten the grains with 3–4 handfuls of water, aerate as before and leave, this time for 10–15 minutes, until the water is absorbed. Rub again to break down any lumps, transfer for a second time to the couscoussière and steam for about 15–20 minutes. Remove the grains and spread over the tray or pan. Sprinkle with salt at this stage. Repeat the whole process one more time then spread the grains over a serving dish and mix in oil or butter,

Mint tea has become Morocco's national drink, but there are also many local tea preparations flavoured with scented herbs or spices, depending on the region. The Moroccans use green tea and add saffron, absinthe (wormwood), mint, cloves, orange blossom, and in winter, *Ras al-hanout (see page 16),* which helps provide warmth.

Green tea is highly beneficial – its caffeine is negligible and does not affect the nervous system; it raises the metabolism, keeps fat burning and is rich in substances that may prevent the growth of cancer cells.

To make a cup of green tea, place ¾–1 teaspoon of green tea leaves in a cup. Boil the water, wait 3 minutes then pour it over the tea and leave to infuse for 1–5 minutes. To add more fragrance, put a few fresh mint leaves into the cup. The tea is best drunk without sugar.

using the back of a wooden spoon to gently break down any lumps. Depending on the recipe, stock, honey or milk may be added at this stage. To serve, pile the cooked couscous into a pyramid shape and accompany with whatever the recipe calls for.

If you do not have a couscoussière, put the couscous in a sieve and rest it over boiling water or a stew, then cook as above. The sieve must be positioned well above the hot water so that only steam reaches the grains and they don't become wet.

Barley couscous is steamed twice, each time for 30 minutes, following the preparation above. Nowadays, many varieties of vegetables or dried fruit are invariably added to couscous, so let your imagination flow and experiment with couscous.

MINT TEA

Tea is very popular and at every occasion, tea infused with mint is offered as a form of greeting and served as an accompaniment to the relaxing moments of the day. In the midst of Moroccan souks and rural streets, silver or copper trays carrying glasses filled with mint tea sweetened with many lumps of sugar are passed around from stalls and in cafés to soothe dry mouths.

STORECUPBOARD INGREDIENTS

ARGAN OIL This comes from the fruit of the argan tree (*Argan spinosa*), which grows in southwestern Morocco. It is rich in vitamin E and polyunsaturated fatty acids and has a strong flavour of hazelnut combined with a faint taste of mature cheese.

Argan oil is used in salads and is delicious with couscous or sweet peppers, or sprinkled on cooked dishes. It is also used to make *Amlou*, a Berber delicacy in which finely chopped toasted almonds are kneaded to a smooth shiny consistency with argan oil and honey. This butter is highly prized. The best argan oil is cold-pressed; always buy it from a reputable store.

CINNAMON There are two types of cinnamon. True cinnamon is the inner bark of the tropical evergreen cinnamon tree dried and curled to form quills. It is light brown with a smooth surface and a sweetish flavour. It is widely available and mostly used in sweet dishes. The second type is the less expensive cassia, from the same family. Cassia bark is dark brown and thick with a rough texture and strong yet subtle flavour. Cassia bark and ground cassia are extensively used in Middle Eastern and North African cuisines, in savoury dishes and sweets. Both cinnamon and cassia are used in *Ras al-hanout (see page 16)*.

CLARIFIED BUTTER This is butter from which the milk solids have been removed. Because of this, it is purer than normal butter and can be heated to much higher temperatures. It will keep, refrigerated, for months. To prepare, *see page 18*.

COUSCOUS Couscous is the staple food of North Africa and is used in many savoury and sweet dishes. It is made from hard wheat moistened with lightly salted water and a little flour. It is then rolled and sieved into fine, medium or large (coarse) pellets and traditionally dried in the sun, although today couscous is mostly sold ready made. Couscous is steamed over the aromatic stew that accompanies it.

Barley couscous, *belboula*, is made from cracked or crushed barley or barley grits and is the traditional couscous of the Berbers in the south of Morocco. It is used in soups and in many couscous dishes, such as *Urkimen (see page 190)*. *Belboula* is sold in Moroccan shops in its raw state or precooked.

Maize couscous is generally eaten with Fish Tagine with Couscous *(see page 174)*. *Beddaz*, a speciality of the region of Ourzazate, is a maize couscous dish in which the leaves of turnips are boiled until tender, drained, thinly sliced and placed over the couscous grains.

In Morocco couscous is eaten by forming a little of it into a ball, using three fingers of the right hand and then conveying it to the mouth.

CUBEB CITRONELLE The berries of a climbing shrub, cubeb have a pungent, spicy flavour and some have a hint of lemon. This spice is very much appreciated in

Morocco and is used in the mixture of spices for *Ras al-hanout (see page 16)*.

FRUCTOSE OR FRUIT SUGAR This comes from honey and from fruit and is lower in calories than table sugar and sweeter, so less is needed. Add it towards the end of cooking time; depending on the brand, it may become bitter if it simmers for a long period. Pure fructose sugar is available in health food shops – make sure you buy a good brand.

FRUIT OF THE ASH TREE (*FRAXINUS*) The fruit has silver-grey bark and feather-like foliage. Its clustered winged seeds are known in Morocco as *Lissanel-tair* (the tongue of the bird). It is included in the mixture of spices for *Ras al-hanout (see page 16)*.

GRAINS OF PARADISE (*AFRAMOMUM MELEGUETTA, MANIGUETTE*) This pungent, peppery spice originates from West Africa and is related to the ginger family. It is used in *Ras al-hanout (see page 16)*.

LONG PEPPER (*PIPER LONGUM*) This spice originated in southern Asia. It has a strong flavour similar to black pepper and is included in the mixture for *Ras al-hanout (see page 16)*.

MALLOW (*MALVA SYLVESTRIS*) This prolific plant originated from the Mediterranean region, but now grows throughout the world. In Morocco, where it is very much appreciated, it is known as *Bekkoula* and the leaves are used in savoury dishes.

MASTIC (*GUM ARABIC*) A resin that comes from the trunk of the *Pistacia lentiscus* tree, native to the eastern Mediterranean. In Morocco it is used to flavour milk puddings and in *Ras al-hanout (see page 16)*. Only a small amount is needed to add its unique flavour.

MINT Several varieties grow in abundance in Morocco and it is widely used to flavour salads and also added to bread and galettes, especially in eastern and northern parts of Morocco. It is also made into mint tea. Mint goes beautifully with tomatoes, aubergines, beetroots and carrots; it flavours yogurt and cucumber salad, and is ideal with fresh or dried fruit salads and watermelon.

ORANGE FLOWER WATER This is the essence distilled from the blossoms of the Seville orange, *Citrus aurantium*. It is very fragrant and in Morocco is used in salads, tagines and sweets. It is also added to the water for washing hands before and after eating.

POMEGRANATE SYRUP This is made by boiling the juice from pomegranate seeds until it becomes a thick syrup. It can be made with sweet or sour pomegranates. The sour syrup is generally used to complement the flavour of certain vegetables, particularly aubergines, meat dishes, such as Shreds of Lamb in Pomegranate Juice *(see page 146)* and some salads. The sweet syrup is used in drinks.

ROSEWATER This is a fragrant essence distilled from the damask rose, *Rosa damascena*. Rosewater is used a lot in sweets and sweet pastries as well as some rice dishes and in many regions of Morocco rose buds are added to the mixture of *Ras al-hanout (see page 16)*.

BASIC RECIPES

CHERMOULA SAUCE

INGREDIENTS 50 g (2 oz) ground coriander │ 2 garlic cloves, peeled │ 1 teaspoon salt │ 2 teaspoons ground cumin │ 1 teaspoon paprika │ ¼ teaspoon cayenne pepper │ ½ teaspoon turmeric │ 1 tablespoon lemon juice │ 1 tablespoon extra virgin olive oil │ 1 ice cube

ONE Blend all the ingredients in a food processor until smooth.

Makes about 100 g (3½ oz)

NUTRIENT ANALYSIS FOR TOTAL 1349 kJ – 324 kcal – 10 g protein – 21 g carbohydrate – 0 g sugars – 24 g fat – 2 g saturates – 0 g fibre – 2.0 g sodium

HARISSA

INGREDIENTS 2 red peppers, cored, deseeded and sliced │ 1–2 mild red chillies, halved and deseeded │ 1 hot chilli, deseeded (optional) │ 2 large garlic cloves │ pinch of salt │ extra virgin olive oil

ONE Dry the peppers and mild chilli in the sun; this might take 1–2 days. Or dry the peppers in a preheated oven, 150°C (300°F) Gas Mark 2, for 15–20 minutes, then reduce the heat to 140°C (275°F) Gas Mark 1 and leave for 30–40 minutes. Remove from the oven and leave to cool. Do the same with the mild chilli, but be careful as it dries very quickly – in 5 minutes or less. **TWO** Put the peppers and mild chillies in a glass jar with the hot chilli, if using, garlic and salt; cover with oil. Seal and leave for 3–4 days. **THREE** Whiz the contents of the jar in a food processor until smooth. Keep the purée in the jar and use as required.

Makes about 250 g (8 oz)

NUTRIENT ANALYSIS PER JAR 1200 kJ – 290 kcal – 4 g protein – 16 g carbohydrate – 12 g sugars – 23 g fat – 3 g saturates – 4 g fibre – 0.01 g sodium (if no salt is added)

RAS AL-HANOUT

INGREDIENTS 15 g (½ oz) dried ginger │ 5 g (¼ oz) long pepper │ 5 g (¼ oz) cinnamon stick │ 5 g (¼ oz) cassia bark │ 5 g (¼ oz) whole nutmeg │ 3 star anise │ 5 g (¼ oz) cardamom │ 5 g (¼ oz) white peppercorns │ 5 g (¼ oz) juniper berries │ 7 cloves │ 7–10 small pieces of mastic (gum arabic) │ 5 g (¼ oz) cubeb citronelle │ 5 g (¼ oz) ground mace │ 5 g (¼ oz) grains of paradise (maniguette) │ 5 g (¼ oz) fruit of the ash tree │ 1 tablespoon turmeric │ 5 g (¼ oz) galangal

ONE Put all the ingredients into an electric grinder and whiz to a powder.

Makes about 60 g (2½ oz)

NUTRIENT ANALYSIS PER JAR 290 kJ – 70 kcal – 4 g protein – 13 g carbohydrate – 3 g sugars – 5 g fat – 2 g saturates – 0 g fibre – 0.01 g sodium

PRESERVED LEMONS

In Morocco only the rind is used, in dishes such as *Tangia*, *Beqqoula*, Tagine of Chicken and Olives and so on. The rind is cut into 5 mm (¼ inch) widths and the pulp is discarded. Rinse the preserved lemon before use.

INGREDIENTS 8 small unwaxed lemons (navel lemons, if possible) | 5 teaspoons sea salt | juice of 1 large lemon

ONE Scrub the lemons under running water, then soak in cold water for 1 hour. Rinse and dry with kitchen paper. **TWO** Cut each lemon into quarters lengthways, from the point to about three-quaters of the way down, leaving them joined at the base. **THREE** Using a long-handled teaspoon, stuff the centre of each lemon with ½ teaspoon of salt, then pinch the sides together. Arrange the lemons upright, packed tightly together, in a sterilized jar. Shake in the remaining salt and lemon juice, then place a weight on top. Alternatively, cover the lemons with warm water. **FOUR** Seal the jar and store in a dry dark place for 3–4 weeks before using.

Makes about 875 g (1¾ lb)

NUTRIENT ANALYSIS PER JAR 600 kJ – 144 kcal – 8 g protein – 25 g carbohydrate – 25 g sugars – 2 g fat – 1 g saturates – 34 g fibre – 9.9 g sodium

CLARIFIED BUTTER

INGREDIENTS 225 g (7½ oz butter)

ONE Put the butter in a pan and place over a medium heat for 1–2 minutes until it melts and starts to bubble. **TWO** Remove the pan from the heat and skim the froth from the surface. **THREE** Carefully pour the clear butter into a bowl, leaving the milk solids in the pan.

Makes 225 g (7 oz)

NUTRIENT ANALYSIS FOR WHOLE AMOUNT 6820 kJ – 1658 kcal – 0 g protein – 0 g carbohydrate – 0 g sugars – 184 g fat – 122 g saturates – 0 g fibre – 0.8 g sodium (for salted butter), 0 g sodium (for unsalted butter)

AROMATIC TOMATO SAUCE

INGREDIENTS 1.2 kg (2¼ lb) tomatoes, skinned, deseeded and chopped | 1 teaspoon salt | ½ teaspoon saffron threads | 125 g (4 oz) onions, grated | 1½ tablespoons extra virgin olive oil | ¼ teaspoon black pepper | ¼–½ teaspoon cayenne pepper | handful of finely chopped parsley or coriander leaves

ONE Stir the tomatoes, salt, saffron, onions and oil together in a pan and simmer until thickened to a medium-thick consistency. **TWO** Sprinkle with the pepper, cayenne and parsley or coriander and simmer for a further 1–2 minutes.

Serves 6

NUTRIENT ANALYSIS PER SERVING 88 kJ – 68 kcal – 2 g protein – 8 g carbohydrate – 7 g sugars – 4 g fat – 1 g saturates – 3 g fibre – 0.4 g sodium

SOUPS

FISH SOUP

This fish soup has wonderful aromas from the colourful variety of vegetables and spices used, and tastes great the following day. Any other white fish, prawns or salmon can be used.

INGREDIENTS ½ tablespoon extra virgin olive oil │ 125 g (4 oz) onions, finely chopped │ 4 garlic cloves, chopped │ good pinch of saffron threads │ 2 tomatoes, chopped │ 1 teaspoon salt, or to taste │ 1.8 litres (3 pints) water │ 1.1 kg (2 lb 2 oz) sea bass with head, scaled and gutted │ ½ teaspoon black pepper │ pinch of nutmeg │ bouquet garni: 2 bay leaves, ½ lemon, a few black peppercorns, 5 parsley sprigs │ 40 g (1½ oz) celery, finely diced │ 125 g (4 oz) fennel, coarsely grated │ 2 carrots, coarsely grated │ ½–¾ teaspoon turmeric │ handful of finely chopped coriander leaves

ONE Heat the oil in a medium pan and sauté the onions and garlic for 1–2 minutes. Crumble in the saffron and stir, then add the tomatoes and ½ teaspoon of the salt and simmer over a low heat for 2–3 minutes. Add 600 ml (1 pint) of the water and bring to the boil, then reduce the heat and simmer for 10–15 minutes. **TWO** Transfer the mixture to a blender or liquidizer and whiz until smooth. **THREE** Rinse the fish and pat dry, then rub inside and out with the remaining salt and sprinkle the cavity with a pinch of the pepper and nutmeg. Remove the fish head. Slice the fish into 3 pieces. **FOUR** Put the bouquet garni in a large pan with the fish head and pieces on top. Add the remaining water and place over a medium heat, skimming off any scum with a slotted spoon. Add the tomato mixture and bring to the boil. Add the celery, fennel and carrots, reduce the heat and cook gently for 5 minutes or until the fish is cooked. Transfer the fish to a dish. **FIVE** Simmer the vegetables and fish head for a further 8–10 minutes, then remove the fish head and add the remaining pepper, the turmeric and coriander. Bone the fish, return it to the stock and simmer gently for 1 minute. Squeeze in the juice from the lemon. Serve the soup hot with bread and olives.

Serves 4–6

NUTRIENT ANALYSIS PER SERVING 986 kJ – 235 kcal – 38 g protein – 7 g carbohydrate – 6 g sugars – 7 g fat – 1 g saturates – 2 g fibre – 0.6 g sodium (if using 1 teaspoon salt)

PUMPKIN SOUP

Here is a delicious, colourful soup inspired by a meaty pumpkin soup that Jewish people in Marrakech prepare for their Easter feast.

INGREDIENTS: 1.2 kg (2¼ lb) peeled pumpkin, deseeded and cut into chunks │ 250 g (8 oz) sweet potato, cut into chunks │ 1.2 litres (2 pints) water │ 1 onion, halved │ 1 cinnamon stick │ 2 large garlic cloves │ 2 teaspoons salt, or to taste │ 3 tablespoons extra virgin olive oil │ 75 g (3 oz) dried chickpeas, soaked, drained and precooked *(see page 29)* │ large handful of fresh or frozen broad beans, skinned │ 1 teaspoon turmeric │ good pinch of black pepper │ 4–5 tablespoons thick natural yogurt │ large handful of finely chopped parsley or mint

ONE Put the pumpkin and sweet potato in a pan and add the water, onion, cinnamon stick, garlic, salt and ½ tablespoon of the oil. Bring to the boil, then reduce the heat to medium-low and simmer for 10–15 minutes until tender. **TWO** Remove and discard the cinnamon stick. Transfer the mixture to a blender or liquidizer and whiz until smooth (you may have to do this in 2 batches), or rub through a sieve. Pour the soup back into the pan, add the chickpeas (if wished, skin before adding) and broad beans and simmer over a medium-low heat. **THREE** Put 1½ tablespoons of the remaining oil, the turmeric and pepper in a small bowl, add the yogurt and stir until smooth. Stir this into the pumpkin mixture and mix well, then leave to simmer for 5–7 minutes, stirring occasionally. **FOUR** Meanwhile, heat a small frying pan, add the remaining oil and the parsley, stir for a few seconds and remove from the heat. (If using mint, do not sauté; just mix into the hot oil.) **FIVE** To serve, pour the soup into a large bowl and stir in the parsley or mint. Alternatively, pour into individual bowls and add 1 tablespoon of the parsley or mint to each. Eat with a good crusty bread.

Serves 4

NUTRIENT ANALYSIS PER SERVING 1299 kJ – 310 kcal – 12 g protein – 35 g carbohydrate – 13 g sugars – 15 g fat – 4 g saturates – 7 g fibre – 1 g sodium (if using 2 teaspoons salt)

VEGETARIAN HARIRA SOUP

INGREDIENTS 50 g (2 oz) dried chickpeas, soaked overnight │ 1.5–1.8 litres (2½–3 pints) water │ 50 g (2 oz) brown lentils │ 50 g (2 oz) brown basmati rice, rinsed once and drained │ 25 g (1 oz) split dried broad beans, soaked for 10 minutes and drained │ 1 onion, finely chopped │ 75 g (3 oz) celery, with leaves if possible, finely diced │ 1 courgette, finely diced │ 1 carrot, finely diced │ 175 g (6 oz) peeled pumpkin, deseeded and finely diced │ 2 tablespoons extra virgin olive oil │ pinch of saffron threads │ 1 teaspoon turmeric │ 2 teaspoons tomato purée │ 500 g (1 lb) tomatoes, skinned, deseeded and finely diced │ 1 tablespoon white flour │ 2 large handfuls of finely chopped coriander leaves │ 2 large handfuls of finely chopped parsley, plus extra sprigs to garnish │ 1½ teaspoons salt, or to taste │ good pinch of black pepper │ about ½ teaspoon freshly grated root ginger │ lemon juice (optional) │ 2–4 lemon wedges │ parsley sprigs, to garnish

ONE Drain the chickpeas and rinse well, then put them in a large pan with the water. Bring slowly to the boil, skimming the surface as foam forms, then reduce the heat to low, cover and simmer for 1½–2 hours or until the chickpeas are very soft. **TWO** Add the lentils, cover and simmer for 10 minutes. Add the rice, broad beans, onion, celery, courgette, carrot and pumpkin, cover and simmer for 20 minutes. **THREE** Meanwhile, heat 1 tablespoon of the oil in a medium pan, add the saffron, a pinch of the turmeric and the tomato purée and stir. Add the tomatoes, breaking them up with the back of a wooden spoon and simmer for 1–2 minutes before adding to the soup. Bring to the boil, then reduce the heat to low, cover and simmer for 15–20 minutes. **FOUR** About 5 minutes before the end of cooking time, ladle 1–2 tablespoons of the soup stock into a bowl and stir in the flour until smooth. Stir this into the soup, adding the remaining oil, the coriander and parsley, then season with the salt, the remaining turmeric, pepper and ginger. **FIVE** Taste and adjust the seasonings. Serve hot, sprinkled with a little lemon juice, if using, with the lemon wedges, garnished with parsley sprigs.

Serves 4–6

NUTRIENT ANALYSIS PER SERVING 1126 kJ – 267 kcal – 11 g protein – 40 g carbohydrate – 10 g sugars – 8 g fat – 1 g saturates – 6 g fibre – 0.8 g sodium (if using 1½ teaspoons salt)

HEALTHY TIP This soup is a mine of nutrients and protein, which strengthen the immune system, give a glow to the skin, feed the nervous system and are excellent for pre-menopausal women. It detoxes the whole body.

recipe illustrated on pages 30–31

HARIRA

During Ramadan, at the setting of the sun the fast is broken with Harira. It is traditionally served with lemon wedges, dates and *Chebakia* (honeyed cakes), but could be served as a one-pot meal, followed by some fresh fruit.

INGREDIENTS 100 g (3½ oz) dried chickpeas, soaked overnight │ 1.8 litres (3 pints) water │ 1½ tablespoons extra virgin olive oil │ 275 g (9 oz) lamb (leg, shoulder or neck), finely diced │ 1 cinnamon stick │ 1 bay leaf │ 75 g (3 oz) brown lentils │ 50 g (2 oz) split dried broad beans, soaked for 10 minutes and drained │ 500 g (1 lb) tomatoes │ 250 g (8 oz) onions, finely chopped │ 275 g (9 oz) celery, finely chopped │ 65 g (2½ oz) coriander leaves, finely chopped │ 65 g (2½ oz) parsley, finely chopped │ 1 teaspoon turmeric │ ½ tablespoon black pepper │ ½ teaspoon saffron threads │ ½ teaspoon ground ginger │ 1½ teaspoons salt, or to taste │ 1 heaped teaspoon tomato purée │ 25 g (1 oz) brown rice │ 2 tablespoons unbleached flour │ lemon juice (optional)

ONE Drain the chickpeas and rinse well. Put in a large pan with 1.2 litres (2 pints) of the water and bring slowly to the boil, skimming the surface as foam forms. Reduce the heat, cover and simmer for 60 minutes. **TWO** Meanwhile, heat ¼ tablespoon of the oil in a frying pan and sauté the lamb for 1–2 minutes. Add to the chickpeas with the cinnamon stick, bay leaf, lentils and broad beans and bring to the boil. Reduce the heat, cover and simmer for a further 30 minutes. **THREE** Meanwhile, purée the tomatoes in a food processor until smooth. **FOUR** Heat the remaining oil in a medium pan and sauté the onions for 2–3 minutes, then add the celery and sauté for 2 minutes until translucent, but do not colour. Stir in the coriander, parsley, turmeric, pepper, saffron, ginger, salt and tomato purée and stir well. Add the puréed tomatoes and 450 ml (¾ pint) of the remaining water. Pour this mixture into the chickpeas and lamb, add the rice and bring to the boil. Reduce the heat, cover and simmer for 30 minutes. **FIVE** Meanwhile, place the flour in a bowl and add the remaining water, whisking continuously. About 15 minutes before the end of cooking time, stir the mixture into the chickpeas and lamb and keep stirring until it boils, then reduce the heat and simmer for the remainder of the cooking time. **SIX** Taste and adjust the seasonings. Serve hot, sprinkled with a little lemon juice, if using.

Serves 4–6

NUTRIENT ANALYSIS PER SERVING 1908 kJ – 453 kcal – 32 g protein – 52 g carbohydrate – 10 g sugars – 15 g fat – 4 g saturates – 9 g fibre – 0.9 g sodium (if using 1½ teaspoons salt)
HEALTHY TIP Harira is rich in protein, an important immunity builder, and also in fibre. It is excellent for diabetics and helps to prevent diabetes, since its sugars are released very slowly into the bloodstream.

BARLEY SEMOLINA SOUP

INGREDIENTS 1.8 litres (3 pints) water | 5 large garlic cloves | 1 teaspoon salt, or to taste | 250 g (8 oz) barley semolina | 300 ml (½ pint) semi-skimmed milk | 2–3 heaped tablespoons thyme leaves | 3 tablespoons extra virgin olive oil | ½ teaspoon black pepper

ONE Place the water and garlic in a large pan and bring to the boil, then reduce the heat to medium-low. Cook for 1 minute, then transfer the garlic to a plate, discard the skin, add ½ teaspoon of the salt and pound to a cream. Stir this into the pan with the barley semolina and simmer, stirring occasionally, until it boils and reaches a thick consistency. **TWO** Gradually stir in the milk and bring to the boil, then reduce the heat and simmer for 8–10 minutes, stirring occasionally. **THREE** Meanwhile, gently crush the thyme with a little of the remaining salt in a mortar with a pestle. Heat a small frying pan, add the oil, turn off the heat and stir in the thyme – it should sizzle. This should be done quickly without burning the thyme. **FOUR** Sprinkle the soup with the pepper, then taste and adjust the salt. Stir the oil and thyme into the soup and serve, or, alternatively, serve the soup in individual bowls and drizzle some oil and thyme over each.

Serves 6

NUTRIENT ANALYSIS PER SERVING 957 kJ – 226 kcal – 5 g protein – 38 g carbohydrate – 3 g sugars – 7 g fat – 1 g saturates – 3 g fibre – 0.4 g sodium (if using 1 teaspoon salt)

BROAD BEAN SOUP

Bissara is a famous purée of broad beans infused with garlic that is served all over Morocco, especially for breakfast, with bread, although in Fez and Meknès it is eaten at any time of the day. Here, I have added more water to turn it into a soup. It is an economical dish, as well as being substantial and strengthening. For vegetarians it is important to include other types of beans and/or nuts in order to provide extra protein. Serve with a tomato and onion salad or any other salad rich in vitamin C, which will aid the absorption of iron.

INGREDIENTS 275 g (9 oz) split dried broad beans, soaked for 10 minutes and drained │ 1–1.2 litres (1¾–2 pints) water │ 12 garlic cloves │ 1¾ teaspoons salt, or to taste │ 3 tablespoons extra virgin olive oil │ 1 teaspoon ground cumin │ 1 teaspoon paprika │ a little chopped mint (optional) │ chilli pepper (optional)

ONE Rinse the broad beans and place with the water in a large pan over a medium heat. Bring slowly to the boil, skimming the surface as foam forms. Add the garlic, then reduce the heat to low, cover and simmer for 15–20 minutes or until the beans are soft. Sprinkle with the salt and remove from the heat. **TWO** Transfer the mixture to a blender or liquidizer and whiz until smooth and creamy (you may have to do this in batches), or rub through a sieve. Pour back into the pan and reheat for 1–2 minutes. **THREE** Meanwhile, mix together the oil, cumin and paprika in a small bowl until smooth. **FOUR** Pour the soup into a large bowl or individual bowls and spoon over the oil mixture and a pinch of mint and chilli pepper, if using. Eat with a good wholemeal bread or croûtons.

Serves 4–6

NUTRIENT ANALYSIS PER SERVING 1280 kJ – 307 kcal – 18 g protein – 37 g carbohydrate – 0 g sugars – 9 g fat – 1 g saturates – 8 g fibre – 0.8 g sodium (if using 1¾ teaspoons salt)

HEALTHY TIP This dish is very rich in E and B vitamins, iron, fibre and sulphur and is excellent for diabetics or those with high blood pressure. Garlic is a powerful antibiotic, nerve calmer, rejuvenator and is known as an aphrodisiac – substances in garlic stimulate the sex glands. The great physician Dioscorides praised it highly.

recipe illustrated on pages 38–39

PUREED CHICKPEA SOUP

I love the thick purée of chickpeas you find in Morocco and here I have added a little more water to produce a soothing and nourishing soup. It is simple and quick to prepare. Authentically, the chickpeas are skinned, which is not difficult to do, but keeping the skins on saves time and increases their fibre content.

INGREDIENTS 250 g (8 oz) dried chickpeas, soaked overnight, or 650 g (1 lb 5 oz) canned chickpeas, drained and rinsed │ 1.5 litres (2½ pints) water │ 1 garlic clove │ 1 small–medium onion, chopped │ ½ teaspoon saffron threads │ 15 g (½ oz) butter or 1 tablespoon extra virgin olive oil │ ½ teaspoon ground or freshly grated root ginger │ 1 teaspoon salt, or to taste │ lemon wedges (optional)

ONE Drain the chickpeas and rinse well. Put them in a pan with the water and bring slowly to the boil, skimming the surface as foam forms. Reduce the heat, cover and simmer for 2 hours or until the chickpeas are soft. If using canned chickpeas, bring the water to the boil, then add the chickpeas with the ingredients at step two. **TWO** Add the garlic, onion, saffron and butter or oil and bring to the boil, then reduce the heat, cover and simmer for 30–40 minutes. **THREE** Remove the pan from the heat and stir in the ginger and salt. Transfer the mixture to a blender or liquidizer and whiz until smooth, or rub through a sieve. Serve hot, with the lemon wedges, if using, and eat with wholemeal croûtons.

Serves 4–6

NUTRIENT ANALYSIS PER SERVING 990 kJ – 235 kcal – 14 g protein – 33 g carbohydrate – 3 g sugars – 7 g fat – 2 g saturates – 9 g fibre – 0.5 g sodium

HEALTHY TIP Chickpeas are naturally rich in protective compounds and phyto-nutrients and are also high in protein, B vitamins and iron. Eating chickpeas on a regular basis benefits the nerves and the heart.

SALADS

COUSCOUS AND MINT SALAD

Argan oil gives the salad a lovely nutty flavour, but if it is not available, olive oil is an excellent substitute.

INGREDIENTS 200 g (7 oz) organic couscous │ 2 tablespoons argan or extra virgin olive oil │ 1–1½ tablespoons dried mint │ 3 tomatoes, skinned, deseeded and finely diced │ 1 large garlic clove, crushed │ 1 onion or 4 small spring onions, finely chopped │ 3 tablespoons lemon juice │ ¼ teaspoon cayenne pepper

ONE Cover the couscous with water. Rake it through with your fingers, then drain and immediately spread it evenly over a large tray. Rake the grains with your fingers a few times to aerate them, then leave for 20–30 minutes until the water is absorbed and the couscous is relatively dry. **TWO** Rub the couscous gently between your palms, letting it fall back into the tray, to break down any lumps. Repeat until the couscous has no lumps. **THREE** Rub your palms with a little of the oil and repeat the process. Alternatively, drizzle the oil over the couscous and rake through the grains. **FOUR** Rub in the mint well, then add the remaining ingredients, mixing gently yet thoroughly. Leave for 5 minutes to let the flavours blend, then serve.

Serves 4–6

NUTRIENT ANALYSIS PER SERVING 752 kJ – 180 kcal – 4 g protein – 29 g carbohydrate – 2g sugars – 6 g fat – 1 g saturates – 1 g fibre – 0.007 g sodium

BEETROOT SALAD

INGREDIENTS 500 g (1 lb 2 oz) beetroot, with skin on ┃ 1 garlic clove ┃ pinch of salt, or to taste ┃ 3–4 mint leaves ┃ 1 heaped tablespoon chopped coriander ┃ ½ tablespoon thyme ┃ 1 teaspoon honey ┃ 1 teaspoon fructose (fruit sugar) ┃ 1 teaspoon extra virgin olive oil ┃ juice of ½ orange ┃ 3 clementines, broken into segments ┃ ¾–1 tablespoon orange flower water ┃ 1 tablespoon parsley, finely chopped

ONE Wash the beetroot and place in a steamer with a close-fitting lid. Steam until tender then remove and allow to cool. **TWO** Peel the beetroot and cut into small cubes. Put the garlic, salt, mint, coriander and thyme in a mortar. Pound with the pestle until it reaches a creamy consistency, then incorporate the honey, fructose (fruit sugar), oil and orange juice. **THREE** Place the beetroot and clementine segments (do not remove their skin), flower water and parsley in a serving bowl, drizzle over the dressing, then toss together and serve.

Serves 4

NUTRIENT ANALYSIS PER SERVING 338 kJ – 80 kcal – 11 g protein – 63 g carbohydrate – 59 g sugars – 1 g fat – 1 g saturates – 4 g fibre – 0.09 g sodium (if no salt is added)

GRATED CARROT AND ORANGE SALAD

A delicious, refreshing and nutritious salad, ideal at any time of the day or on any occasion. I have added some pine nuts for extra flavour and have substituted honey for sugar, since honey is rich in mineral salts and its health-giving properties have been known since ancient times.

INGREDIENTS 1 tablespoon dark honey │ 1 tablespoon orange flower water │ 3 tablespoons lemon juice │ 2–3 tablespoons orange juice │ 1 tablespoon ground or grated almonds │ ½ teaspoon salt │ 500 g (1 lb) carrots, grated │ 2 oranges, each peeled and cut into 8–10 pieces │ 1 teaspoon extra virgin olive oil │ 2 tablespoons pine nuts │ mint leaves, to garnish (optional)

ONE Put the honey in a serving dish, then mix in the flower water and lemon and orange juices. Add the almonds, salt, carrots and oranges. **TWO** Heat the oil in a small pan and sauté the pine nuts until golden, then remove them from the pan and add to the salad. **THREE** Toss the salad, garnish with mint, if wished, and serve, or chill for later use.

Serves 4–5

NUTRIENT ANALYSIS PER SERVING 818 kJ – 196 kcal – 4 g protein – 26 g carbohydrate – 25 g sugars – 9 g fat – 1 g saturates – 5 g fibre – 0.3 g sodium

HEALTHY TIP Rich in fibre, this salad contains a wealth of vitamins as well as powerful antioxidants, betacarotene (pro-vitamin A) and vitamin C, both of which protect the body and help to keep degenerative diseases at bay.

recipe illustrated on pages 50–51

HARICOT BEAN SALAD

I first ate this fresh-tasting salad when visiting the graceful Imperial city of Meknès. It came accompanied by potato and courgette salads and briouats with chicken *(see page 226, but these are made with lamb)*. Once the beans have been soaked, it is simple to make. In Morocco, they boil the soaked beans for a few minutes, then drain them, cover with fresh water and cook them until soft. This is said to cut down on their gas.

INGREDIENTS 200 g (7 oz) dried haricot beans, soaked for 6 hours │ 450 ml (¾ pint) water │ 65 g (2½ oz) onions, grated │ piece of fresh root ginger │ 125 g (4 oz) tomatoes, skinned, deseeded and sliced into chunks │ ½ tablespoon extra virgin olive oil │ ½ teaspoon turmeric │ 2 teaspoons organic apple cider vinegar │ ½ teaspoon salt │ pinch of black pepper │ flat leaf parsley sprigs, to garnish (optional)

ONE Drain the beans and rinse well, then put them in a pan with the water. Bring slowly to the boil, skimming the surface as foam forms, then reduce the heat to very low, cover and simmer for 20 minutes. **TWO** Add the onions, ginger, tomatoes and oil and simmer, covered, for 15 minutes until the beans are tender. **THREE** A few minutes before the end of the cooking time, mash the tomatoes against the side of the pan, then add the turmeric, vinegar, salt and pepper. Remove the pan from the heat, cover and leave until it reaches room temperature, then remove the piece of ginger. Serve, garnished with parsley sprigs, if wished.

Serves 2–4

NUTRIENT ANALYSIS PER SERVING 1436 kJ – 338 kcal – 23 g protein – 57 g carbohydrate – 9 g sugars – 4 g fat – 1 g saturates – 25 g fibre – 0.8 g sodium

HEALTHY TIP Haricot beans are rich in calcium, magnesium, chromium, copper, iron and fibre as well as the B vitamins.

recipe illustrated on pages 54–55

CUCUMBER AND NUT SALAD

INGREDIENTS 4–6 mint leaves | about 1 tablespoon thyme leaves | 3–4 paper-thin slices of garlic | ½ tablespoon icing sugar | 1 heaped tablespoon shelled pistachio nuts | 2 teaspoons pine nuts | 1 tablespoon extra virgin olive oil | ½–¾ teaspoon salt, or to taste | ½ tablespoon lime juice | ¾ tablespoon lemon juice | 500 g (1 lb) cucumber, unpeeled | I tablespoon orange flower water, or to taste | pinch of black pepper

ONE To make the dressing, put the mint, thyme, garlic, icing sugar and pistachio and pine nuts in a mortar and pound with a pestle until very creamy. **TWO** Gradually incorporate the oil, salt and lime and lemon juices. **THREE** Coarsely grate the cucumber into a bowl, add the flower water and toss with the dressing and pepper. This will keep for up to 2 days in the refrigerator.

Serves 4

NUTRIENT ANALYSIS PER SERVING 469 kJ – 113 kcal – 3 g protein – 5 g carbohydrate – 4 g sugars – 9 g fat – 1 g saturates – 1 g fibre – 0.3 g sodium

HEALTHY TIP This salad contains E and C vitamins and has oils that feed the brain and hydrate the skin, while thyme is an excellent hair strengthener – in fact, this should really be called a beauty salad. To increase the nutrients, add some watercress, which is high in antioxidants and also anti-ageing.

LENTIL SALAD

INGREDIENTS 150 g (5 oz) brown lentils | 300 ml (½ pint) water | ½ teaspoon salt, or to taste | 1 large garlic clove, unpeeled | 65 g (2½ oz) onion | 1 tablespoon extra virgin olive oil | ½ teaspoon ground ginger or freshly grated root ginger | 1½ tablespoons lemon juice | ½ teaspoon ground cumin | pinch of black pepper | large handful of finely chopped parsley

ONE Place the lentils, water, salt and garlic in a small pan and grate the onion over. Add 1 teaspoon of the oil and the ground or fresh ginger. Bring to the boil, then reduce the heat to low, cover and simmer for 40 minutes or until the lentils are tender (the time will depend on the quality of the lentils). If using a heat diffuser, cook for about 1 hour. **TWO** When the lentils are ready, remove the pan from the heat, discard the garlic skin and mash the garlic pulp against the side of the pan, then mix it into the lentils and leave to cool a little. **THREE** Stir in the lemon juice, cumin, pepper and parsley and serve with a plate of coarsely grated carrots and a Potato, Turmeric and Cumin Salad *(see page 63)*. Put some of the lentils on a plate, sprinkle with shreds of carrot and then top with some of the potato salad.

Serves 4

NUTRIENT ANALYSIS PER SERVING 614 kJ – 145 kcal – 10 g protein – 20 g carbohydrate – 2 g sugars – 4 g fat – 1 g saturates – 1 g fibre – 0.3 g sodium (if using ½ teaspoon salt)

TOMATO, CUCUMBER AND PEPPER SALAD

A nutritious salad that can be consumed throughout the year; it is good with Kefta with Aromatic Herbs *(see page 124)* or served with other salads.

INGREDIENTS 1 garlic clove │ 1 teaspoon salt, or to taste │ 4 mint leaves │ 2 tablespoons lemon juice │ 2 tablespoons extra virgin olive oil │ 40–50 g (1½–2 oz) onion, sliced into rings │ 500 g (1 lb) tomatoes, skinned, deseeded and diced │ 175 g (6 oz) green pepper, cored, deseeded and diced │ 75 g (3 oz) cucumber, unpeeled and diced │ handful of finely chopped parsley │ pinch of black pepper (optional)

ONE To make the dressing, put the garlic, salt and mint in a mortar and pound with a pestle until creamy. Gradually incorporate the lemon juice and oil. **TWO** Put the onion, tomatoes, green pepper, cucumber and parsley in a salad bowl and sprinkle with the pepper, if using. **THREE** Add the dressing and toss well before serving.

Serves 4

NUTRIENT ANALYSIS PER SERVING 365 kJ – 88 kcal – 3 g protein – 6 g carbohydrate – 5 g sugars – 6 g fat – 1 g saturates – 2 g fibre – 0.5 g sodium (if using 1 teaspoon salt)

recipe illustrated on pages 60–61

COURGETTE SALAD

INGREDIENTS 500 g (1 lb) courgettes | 1 tablespoon extra virgin olive oil | 1–2 thyme sprigs or 1 tablespoon dried thyme | 2 garlic cloves, peeled and chopped | ½ teaspoon paprika | ¼ teaspoon turmeric | ½ teaspoon salt, or to taste | ½ teaspoon ground cumin, or to taste | ½ teaspoon icing sugar (optional) | pinch of black pepper | 1 tablespoon lemon juice, or to taste

ONE Steam the courgettes for 4–5 minutes. Leave to cool, then dice. **TWO** Put ½ tablespoon of the oil, the thyme, garlic, paprika and diced courgettes into a small frying pan. Place over a medium heat and shake the pan or gently stir for 1 minute to bring their flavours together. **THREE** Stir in the turmeric, salt, cumin, icing sugar, if using, and pepper. Shake the pan a few times, then remove from the heat and add the lemon juice and remaining oil. Shake the pan once more and serve warm or at room temperature.

Serves 4

NUTRIENT ANALYSIS PER SERVING 215 kJ – 52 kcal – 2 g protein – 3 g carbohydrate – 3 g sugars – 3 g fat – 1 g saturates – 0 g fibre – 0.3 g sodium (if using ½ teaspoon salt)

POTATO, TURMERIC AND CUMIN SALAD

INGREDIENTS 500 g (1 lb) white potatoes, scrubbed and left whole │ 1 teaspoon turmeric │ ½ teaspoon salt, or to taste │ ½–¾ teaspoon ground cumin │ 2 tablespoons extra virgin olive oil

ONE Steam the potatoes for 20–30 minutes (the time will depend on the size and type of potato), then leave them to cool. **TWO** Meanwhile, prepare the dressing. Put the turmeric, salt and cumin in a small bowl and gradually add the oil, then mix thoroughly. **THREE** Using a sharp knife, cut the potatoes into small cubes, then drizzle over the dressing and toss gently. Serve with bread, green olives and a slice of goats', haloumi or kaskaval cheese – the latter two cheeses are not authentic to Morocco, while goats' cheese is.

Serves 4

NUTRIENT ANALYSIS PER SERVING 612 kJ – 146 kcal – 3 g protein – 22 g carbohydrate – 1 g sugars – 6 g fat – 1 g saturates – 2 g fibre – 0.3 g sodium (if using ½ teaspoon salt)

HEALTHY TIP A salad full of vitamin C, magnesium, potassium and curcumin, the powerful antioxidant.

POTATO SALAD WITH HERBS AND TOMATOES

This nutritious salad is simple to prepare and is economical. I had it for lunch in Meknès, one of the four Imperial cities. A whole array of small dishes containing different salads and Briouats *(see pages 216–227)* were served. All were delicious and reminded me of home cooking.

INGREDIENTS 750 g (1½ lb) new or salad potatoes, scrubbed and left whole │ 250 g (8 oz) tomatoes, skinned, deseeded and chopped │ 100 ml (3½ fl oz) water │ 1 teaspoon double-concentrated tomato purée │ I teaspoon salt, or to taste │ 1 small onion, grated │ 1 garlic clove, finely crushed │ ½ teaspoon paprika │ a few saffron threads │ pinch of ground ginger │ 1–1½ tablespoons extra virgin olive oil │ ¼ teaspoon ground cumin │ a little parsley, finely chopped │ a few coriander leaves, finely chopped │ pinch of black pepper │ 1 tablespoon lemon juice │ pinch of cayenne pepper (optional) or ½ teaspoon **Harissa** *(see page 15)*

ONE Steam the potatoes for 20–30 minutes (the time will depend on the size and type of potato), then leave to cool and cut into small cubes. Alternatively, cut the potatoes into cubes and cook them in the tomato sauce *(see step two)* until nearly tender, then add all the other ingredients. **TWO** Put the tomatoes, water, tomato purée, salt, onion, garlic, paprika, saffron, ginger and ½ tablespoon of the oil in a medium frying pan and simmer over a low–medium heat for 5–8 minutes. **THREE** Add the potatoes, cumin, parsley and coriander and shake the pan to mix. Add the remaining oil, sprinkle with pepper and simmer for 1 minute, then add the lemon juice. Give the pan another shake and sprinkle with cayenne pepper, if using, or stir in the Harissa. Serve hot or at room temperature.

Serves 4

NUTRIENT ANALYSIS PER SERVING 848 kJ – 201 kcal – 4 g protein – 34 g carbohydrate – 6 g sugars – 6 g fat – 1 g saturates – 4 g fibre – 0.4 g sodium (if using I teaspoon salt)

HEALTHY TIP This dish is rich in phosphorus, potassium, vitamin C and chromium, which maintains sugar levels in the bloodstream.

recipe illustrated on pages 66–67

BROAD BEAN AND CORIANDER SALAD

This salad is simple, quick to make and very tasty. Fresh broad beans, when in season, are excellent, if you have the patience to skin them, otherwise buy good-quality frozen broad beans. Serve with Orange and Olive Salad *(see page 75)*.

INGREDIENTS 500 g (1 lb) fresh shelled or frozen broad beans │ 3 garlic cloves, unpeeled │ 1¼ tablespoons lemon juice, or to taste │ 1½ tablespoons extra virgin olive oil │ ½–¾ teaspoon salt, or to taste │ black pepper, to taste │ small pinch of ground cumin (optional) │ handful of coriander leaves, finely chopped

ONE Put the shelled fresh broad beans in a steamer with the garlic and steam for 4–5 minutes. If using frozen beans, rinse them slightly to remove any ice, drain and steam for 6–8 minutes. **TWO** Remove from the heat and, if you have the patience, skin the beans (this will take 10–15 minutes). Place in a serving bowl. **THREE** Peel the garlic, mash and mix with the lemon juice and oil. Sprinkle the salt, pepper, cumin, if using, and coriander over the broad beans, then drizzle with the oil mixture. Toss and serve.

Serves 2–4

NUTRIENT ANALYSIS PER SERVING 957 kJ – 230 kcal – 15 g protein – 19 g carbohydrate – 4 g sugars – 11 g fat – 1 g saturates – 2 g fibre – 0.5 g sodium (if using ½ teaspoon salt)

THREE PEPPER SALAD

Placing the peppers on a heat diffuser over a gas flame cooks them in minutes, locking in most of their nutrients and flavour. In Morocco, peppers are much appreciated and are prepared in various ways. They are usually fried and are then generally eaten hot, but grilling them is a much healthier way to cook them. Serve this salad as a starter or to accompany Chicken with Aromatic Spices *(see page 100)* or Poussin in Aromatic Sauce *(see page 94)*.

INGREDIENTS 250 g (8 oz) green peppers │ 250 g (8 oz) red peppers │ 250 g (8 oz) yellow peppers │ 1 small garlic clove │ ½ teaspoon salt, or to taste │ 1 teaspoon organic apple cider vinegar │ 1¼ tablespoons lemon juice │ 1¼–1½ tablespoons extra virgin olive oil │ ¼ teaspoon ground cumin, or to taste │ handful of parsley or coriander leaves, finely chopped │ pinch of black pepper (optional)

ONE Place the peppers on a heat diffuser over a medium gas flame. Turn them for 3–5 minutes to char all over. Alternatively, preheat the grill to high, then grill the peppers for 18 minutes or until charred on all sides. Leave to cool, then skin, core and deseed. Slice the flesh into julienne strips. **TWO** Meanwhile, cream the garlic and salt in a mortar with a pestle. Incorporate the vinegar, lemon juice and oil and add to the peppers. Sprinkle with the cumin, parsley or coriander and pepper, if using. Toss, taste and adjust the seasonings if necessary, then serve.

Serves 4

NUTRIENT ANALYSIS PER SERVING 420 kJ – 100 kcal – 3 g protein – 8 g carbohydrate – 8 g sugars – 6 g fat – 1 g saturates – 3 g fibre – 0.3 g sodium (if using ½ teaspoon salt)

HEALTHY TIP This salad is a mine of cancer-fighting nutrients. It is rich in carotenoids, vitamin C, betacarotene and silicon (good for forming collagen and healthy nails, skin and hair). It is also anti-ageing.

recipe illustrated on pages 72–73

OLIVE SALAD

INGREDIENTS 200 g (7 oz) mixed olives, pitted and rinsed | 1 tablespoon lemon juice | 2 tablespoons orange juice | 1 teaspoon extra virgin olive oil | ½ teaspoon ground cumin | ¼ teaspoon paprika | good pinch of ground ginger | thin shreds of red pepper

ONE Mix the olives with the lemon and orange juices, oil, cumin, paprika and ginger. Toss with the red pepper and serve with bread.

Serves 4

NUTRIENT ANALYSIS PER SERVING 259 kJ – 63 kcal – 1 g protein – 1 g carbohydrate – 1 g sugars – 6 g fat – 1 g saturates – 2 g fibre – 1.1 g sodium

HEALTHY TIP Olives are an excellent food, rich in monounsaturated fats that aid in reducing bad cholesterol. Nevertheless, they should be consumed in moderation, since they are pickled in a lot of salt. Remember to rinse them before use.

ORANGE AND OLIVE SALAD

Here is a very refreshing and nutritious salad, excellent for eating during cold weather.

INGREDIENTS 3 oranges | pinch of salt, or to taste | 75 g (3 oz) black olives, halved, pitted and rinsed | juice of ½–1 orange, to taste | ½–¾ tablespoon extra virgin olive oil | bunch of watercress, leaves and tender stems

ONE Peel and slice each orange, then cut into small–medium pieces. Place in a serving bowl and sprinkle with the salt. **TWO** Add the olives, orange juice and oil and toss. Add the watercress, toss again and serve.

Serves 4

NUTRIENT ANALYSIS PER SERVING 365 kJ – 87 kcal – 2 g protein – 11 g carbohydrate – 11 g sugars – 4 g fat – 1 g saturates – 3 g fibre – 0.4 g sodium

HEALTHY TIP A salad rich in pro-vitamin A and C, B1, B2 and B9 vitamins, potassium, phosphorus, manganese, magnesium, iron and pectin, which helps lower bad cholesterol and combat fatigue, aids digestion and protects from certain cancers. The addition of watercress gives a tasty, peppery note and guards the body against pollution and the effects of smoking.

BEETROOT AND MANGO SALAD

This colourful salad is very refreshing, nutritious and quick to prepare and makes an attractive dish for a buffet.

INGREDIENTS 3–4 small-medium raw beetroot, washed and coarsely grated │ 1–2 mangoes (if possible Indian), cubed │ ¾ teaspoon icing sugar │ 1 small garlic clove │ 10–12 mint leaves │ ½ teaspoon salt │ 2 tablespoons lime juice │ 2 tablespoons thick natural yogurt │ juice of 2 oranges │ 1 tablespoon extra virgin olive oil │ a little over ¼ tablespoon orange flower water

ONE Place the grated beetroot in a mixing bowl and the mangoes in a smaller bowl. Using a small sieve with fine holes, sprinkle the icing sugar over the beetroot and mangoes. **TWO** Pound the garlic, mint and salt in a mortar with a pestle until smooth, then gradually add the lime juice, yogurt, orange juice, oil and flower water. **THREE** Pour a little more than half the sauce over the beetroot and toss. Pour the remaining sauce over the mangoes. **FOUR** Place the beetroot in a serving dish and spread over the mangoes and sauce. Chill for 30 minutes, then serve.

Serves 4

NUTRIENT ANALYSIS PER SERVING 449 kJ – 107 kcal – 3 g protein – 14 g carbohydrate – 13 g sugars – 5 g fat – 2 g saturates – 3 g fibre – 0.3 g sodium

HEALTHY TIP A salad rich in vitamin C, copper, selenium, sulphur and iron. Its potent antioxidants, vitamin C and betacarotene aid in strengthening the body's defences against stomach, breast and other cancers. Beetroot and its leaves and mango have a high content of betacarotene, which beautifies the skin and delays ageing.

recipe illustrated on pages 78–79

COUSCOUS AND BROAD BEAN SALAD

INGREDIENTS 500 g (1 lb) fresh shelled or frozen broad beans │ 2 garlic cloves, unpeeled │ 125 ml (4 fl oz) water │ 50 g (2 oz) onion, grated │ 2 pinches of saffron threads │ pinch of paprika │ 1 teaspoon salt, or to taste │ 2 tablespoons finely chopped coriander leaves │ 1½ tablespoons extra virgin olive oil │ pinch of black pepper │ 2 tablespoons lemon juice │ 300 g (10 oz) organic couscous │ bouquet garni: 2 bay leaves, 1 parsley sprig, 1 coriander sprig │ pinch of turmeric

ONE If using frozen broad beans, rinse them slightly to remove any ice, then drain. Put the beans, garlic, water, onion, 1 pinch of the saffron, paprika and ½ teaspoon of the salt in a medium pan and simmer over a low heat for 5–8 minutes. A minute or two before the end of cooking time add the coriander and ½ tablespoon of the oil, then season with the pepper. Remove from the heat. Peel the garlic, mash until creamy and mix with the bean mixture. Add the lemon juice and leave to cool. **TWO** Meanwhile, cover the couscous with water. Rake it through with your fingers, then drain and immediately spread it evenly over a large tray. Rake the grains with your fingers a few times to aerate them, then leave for 20–30 minutes until the water is absorbed and the couscous is relatively dry. **THREE** Sprinkle the couscous with the remaining salt and rub the grains gently between your palms, allowing it to fall back into the tray, to break down any lumps. **FOUR** Put about 300 ml (½ pint) of water, the bouquet garni, the remaining saffron and turmeric in the lower part of a couscoussière, or in a pan, and bring to the boil. Put the couscous in the perforated top part of the couscoussière, or in a fine sieve, place over the boiling water and steam for about 30 minutes. **FIVE** When the couscous is cooked, put it in a large dish and drizzle over the remaining oil, then, using a fork, mix gently to separate the grains. Add the cooled bean mixture and mix well. Taste and adjust the seasonings, leave for a few minutes to allow the flavours to blend, then serve.

Serves 4

NUTRIENT ANALYSIS PER SERVING 1255 kJ – 300 kcal – 12 g protein – 49 g carbohydrate – 3 g sugars – 8 g fat – 1 g saturates – 5 g fibre – 0.5 g sodium (if using 1 teaspoon salt)

recipe illustrated on pages 82–83

CHICKEN

CHICKEN, COUSCOUS AND ONIONS

Chicken (or lamb or veal) is simmered with aromatic spices, creating a rich stock. The onions are caramelized with butter and honey.

INGREDIENTS 750 ml (1¼ pints) water │ 1 small chicken, cut into 6–8 pieces │ bouquet garni: 1 cinnamon stick, 1 bay leaf, 1 cardamom pod │ 1 medium onion, finely chopped │ 3 garlic cloves, crushed │ good pinch of saffron threads │ 1½ teaspoons salt, or to taste │ ½ teaspoon ground ginger │ ¼ teaspoon black pepper │ 250 g (8 oz) couscous │ 2 tablespoons extra virgin olive oil │ 500 g (1 lb) onions, sliced │ 75 g (3 oz) raisins │ ½ teaspoon ground cinnamon │ small pinch of freshly grated nutmeg │ 1–2 tablespoons dark honey │ a little under ½ tablespoon orange flower water or rosewater (optional)

ONE Put the water and chicken into a medium pan and bring slowly to the boil. Add the bouquet garni, onion, garlic, saffron and 1¼ teaspoons of salt. Reduce the heat, cover and simmer for 50–60 minutes until the chicken is tender. Add the ginger and pepper 5 minutes before the end of cooking. **TWO** Meanwhile, cover the couscous with water. Rake it through with your fingers, then drain and immediately spread it evenly over a large tray. Rake the grains with your fingers a few times to aerate them, then leave for 20–30 minutes until the water is absorbed and the couscous is relatively dry. **THREE** Rub the couscous gently between your palms, letting it fall back into the tray, to break down any lumps. Sprinkle with the remaining salt, drizzle over 1 tablespoon of the oil and rake through the grains. **FOUR** Ladle 300 ml (½ pint) stock from the pan, pour into a small pan and bring to a rapid boil, then turn off the heat and add the couscous. Cover and leave until the stock has been absorbed. **FIVE** Heat the remaining oil in a pan and sauté the onions gently until lightly golden. Ladle 200 ml (7 fl oz) stock into a small bowl. Pour a little stock into the onions and cook until reduced. Repeat until all the stock has been added and reduced. As the onions soften, increase the heat. **SIX** Add the raisins, cinnamon and nutmeg, then the honey and leave to caramelize for 5–10 minutes. Stir in the flower water or rosewater, if using, and turn off the heat. **SEVEN** To serve, put the couscous in a serving dish and top with the onions. Serve the chicken and stock separately.

Serves 4–6

NUTRIENT ANALYSIS PER SERVING 3256 kJ – 780 kcal – 46 g protein – 66 g carbohydrate – 32 g sugars – 39 g fat – 9 g saturates – 3 g fibre – 0.7 g sodium (if using 1 teaspoon of salt)

recipe illustrated on pages 90–91

CHICKEN WITH TOMATOES IN HONEY

As well as being succulent, Moroccan dishes are easy to make. This dish just needs stirring from time to time. It makes a good family meal, or a main course for a dinner party. It can be prepared ahead of time to step four, then the cinnamon and honey can be added to simmer gently for 10–15 minutes just before serving.

INGREDIENTS 1 tablespoon extra virgin olive oil │ handful of blanched almonds │ 4 skinless chicken portions, about 300 g (10 oz) │ 300 g (10 oz) onions, grated or finely chopped │ 5 large tomatoes, skinned, deseeded and coarsely chopped │ ½ teaspoon saffron threads │ good pinch of black pepper │ ½–¾ teaspoon salt │ ½–¾ teaspoon ground cinnamon │ 1 tablespoon dark honey

ONE Heat a pan, add the oil and almonds and sauté until golden in colour. Alternatively, put the almonds on a baking sheet and toast in a preheated oven, 180°C (350°F) Gas Mark 4, for about 10 minutes. Remove and put to one side. **TWO** Add the chicken to the pan, cover and sauté over a medium–high heat for about 5 minutes, stirring occasionally. When the chicken has turned golden in colour, reduce the heat to medium and leave to cook, still covered, in its own juice for a further 15 minutes, stirring from time to time. **THREE** Stir in the onions and cook for a few more minutes, then add the tomatoes, saffron, pepper and salt. Cover and simmer for 40 minutes, stirring once or twice. **FOUR** Transfer the chicken to a side dish and continue simmering the tomatoes until the liquid has almost evaporated. Season with cinnamon and drizzle all over with the honey. **FIVE** Return the chicken to the pan, simmer for a few minutes to warm through, then garnish with the almonds and serve with couscous.

Serves 4

NUTRIENT ANALYSIS PER SERVING 905 kJ – 215 kcal – 19 g protein – 18 g carbohydrate – 16 g sugars – 8 g fat – 2 g saturates – 4 g fibre – 0.3 g sodium

HEALTHY TIP Chicken with tomatoes and honey is a nourishing dish that warms and strengthens the body. It is low in fat and rich in protein, antioxidants, potassium and easily assimilated sugars.

POUSSIN IN AROMATIC SAUCE

INGREDIENTS 2 large garlic cloves | 1 teaspoon salt | 2 tablespoons coriander leaves | ½ teaspoon ground coriander | ¾ teaspoon ground cumin | ¼–½ teaspoon caraway seeds | good pinch of black pepper | 2 tablespoons extra virgin olive oil | 2 tablespoons lemon juice | 1 tablespoon water | ½ teaspoon dark honey | 2 poussins | 500 g (1 lb) potatoes, cut into thick chunks

ONE To make the marinade, put the garlic, salt and coriander leaves in a mortar and pound with a pestle until smooth. **TWO** Add the ground coriander, cumin, caraway and pepper and mix to a creamy consistency, then gradually add the oil, lemon juice, water and honey and stir to mix. **THREE** Slice each poussin along its backbone, open out and, using the heel of your hand, flatten the bird. Rub the poussins all over with some of the marinade, then rub the potatoes with the remaining marinade. Cover and refrigerate overnight. **FOUR** Put the poussin and potatoes in a baking dish and bake in a preheated oven, 180°C (350°F) Gas Mark 4, for 1 hour or until the poussin and potatoes are cooked through and well browned all over.

Serves 2–4

NUTRIENT ANALYSIS PER SERVING 3460 kJ – 828 kcal – 56 g protein – 46 g carbohydrate – 4 g sugars – 48 g fat – 11 g saturates – 4 g fibre – 1.2 g sodium

CHICKEN TREED

This tasty, extremely healthy dish is said to date from the 7th century and is believed to have been a favourite of the prophet Mohammed. Instead of the pastry, try using a *marqooq* loaf, cut into 8 pieces.

INGREDIENTS 1 tablespoon extra virgin olive oil | 1 medium chicken, skinned and cut into 4–6 pieces, or 4–6 skinless chicken portions | 1.2 litres (2 pints) water | 500 g (1 lb) onions, sliced | 3 garlic cloves, crushed | good pinch of saffron threads | 1 cinnamon stick | 1 bay leaf | I teaspoon ground ginger | 1¼ teaspoons salt, or to taste | 75 g (3 oz) brown lentils | 40 g (1½ oz) split dried broad beans, soaked for 10 minutes and drained | pinch of black pepper | ½ teaspoon turmeric | ½ teaspoon ground cinnamon (optional) | 1 teaspoon icing sugar (optional)

DOUGH 250 g (8 oz) unbleached flour | ½ teaspoon salt | about 150 ml (¼ pint) warm water, or as necessary | 40 ml (1½ fl oz) olive oil, plus extra for oiling

ONE Heat the oil in a pan and sauté the chicken for a few minutes, turning to brown on all sides. Add the water and bring slowly to the boil, skimming the surface as foam forms. Add the onions, garlic, saffron, cinnamon stick, bay leaf, half the ginger, the salt, lentils and broad beans. Reduce the heat to medium-low, cover and simmer for 40–50 minutes or until the chicken is tender. Towards the end of cooking time add the remaining ginger, the pepper and turmeric. **TWO** Meanwhile, make the dough. Put the flour and salt in a bowl, gradually add the water and knead very thoroughly for about 15 minutes. Pinch off pieces of the dough to form 8 small balls, place in a tray with the oil and turn to coat with the oil. Keeping your hands oiled, flatten each ball, pressing down with the heel of your hand and pulling the dough out all round to form a round as thin as possible. **THREE** Heat a heavy nonstick pan, then add one sheet – it will dry immediately. Turn it over to dry the other side (do not brown), then remove from the pan and repeat with the remaining sheets. **FOUR** To serve, place 1 or 2 sheets in each dish and top with some chicken, onions, lentils and beans then ladle over some of the stock. Sprinkle with cinnamon and icing sugar, if using.

Serves 4

NUTRIENT ANALYSIS PER SERVING 2604 kJ – 619 kcal – 46 g protein – 73 g carbohydrate – 9 g sugars – 18 g fat – 4 g saturates – 4 g fibre – 1 g sodium (if using 1¾ teaspoons salt)

HEALTHY TIP This dish is very rich in A, B and E vitamins, phosphorus, iron and zinc, quercetin, selenium and germanium. Whenever I eat it, my sleep is never interrupted.

recipe illustrated on pages 98–99

CHICKEN WITH AROMATIC SPICES

INGREDIENTS 2–3 large garlic cloves | ½–1 teaspoon freshly grated root ginger | 1 tablespoon thyme | 1 teaspoon salt | ¼ teaspoon black pepper | ¼–½ teaspoon turmeric | ¾ tablespoon lemon juice | 1 teaspoon organic apple cider vinegar | 1½ tablespoons extra virgin olive oil | 2 tablespoons water | 500 g (1 lb) boneless, skinless chicken breasts, diced

ONE To make the marinade, cream the garlic, ginger, thyme and salt in a mortar with a pestle, then add the pepper and turmeric. Gradually add the lemon juice, vinegar, oil and water and mix well until smooth. Rub the chicken pieces all over with the marinade, cover and refrigerate overnight. **TWO** Remove the chicken from the refrigerator and leave at room temperature for a few minutes, then put into a baking dish and bake in a preheated oven, 180°C (350°F) Gas Mark 4, for 20 minutes or until browned. Serve with a salad.

Serves 3–5

NUTRIENT ANALYSIS PER SERVING 1063 kJ – 253 kcal – 37 g protein – 2 g carbohydrate – 0 g sugars – 11 g fat – 3 g saturates – 0 g fibre – 0.8 g sodium

TAGINE OF CHICKEN WITH POTATOES AND OLIVES

INGREDIENTS 1 small–medium chicken, cut into 4–6 pieces │ 450 ml (¾ pint) water │ 1–2 bay leaves │ 200 g (7 oz) onions, grated │ 1 teaspoon salt, or to taste │ pinch of saffron threads │ 3 garlic cloves, crushed │ ½ teaspoon ground ginger │ 1 tablespoon extra virgin olive oil │ 1.1 kg (2 lb 2 oz) potatoes, scrubbed and cubed │ large handful of finely chopped coriander leaves │ 2 thyme sprigs │ about 10 black or green olives, pitted and rinsed (optional) │ pinch of black pepper │ 2 tablespoons lemon juice, or to taste

ONE Place the chicken and water in a medium pan and bring slowly to the boil, skimming the surface as foam forms. Add the bay leaves, onions, salt, saffron, garlic, ginger and 1 teaspoon of the oil. Reduce the heat to medium-low and simmer for 25–30 minutes. **TWO** Add the potatoes and continue cooking until they and the chicken are tender, checking the water level and adding a little more hot water if necessary. About 5 minutes before the end of cooking time add the coriander, thyme, olives, if using, pepper and the remaining oil. **THREE** Drizzle all over with the lemon juice and serve with crusty bread and a salad.

Serves 4

NUTRIENT ANALYSIS PER SERVING 1863 kJ – 440 kcal – 40 g protein – 52 g carbohydrate – 5 g sugars – 10 g fat – 2 g saturates – 6 g fibre – 1 g sodium (if using 1 teaspoon salt)

CHICKEN, CHICKPEAS AND RAISINS

This is a comforting and energizing dish. It has subtle flavours in spite of the powerful aroma of saffron. The turmeric bestows a beautiful pale colour on the liquor.

INGREDIENTS 75 g (3 oz) dried chickpeas, soaked overnight, or 400 g (13 oz) can chickpeas, drained and rinsed │ 750 ml (1¼ pints) water │ 2½ small–medium onions │ 1 medium chicken, skinned and cut into 4–6 pieces │ bouquet garni: 1 celery stick, 1 bay leaf, 1 large cinnamon stick │ a few saffron threads │ 50–125 g (2–4 oz) raisins │ ¾ teaspoon turmeric │ 300 g (10 oz) organic couscous │ salt and black pepper

ONE Drain the soaked chickpeas and rinse well. Put them in a medium pan with the water and bring slowly to the boil, skimming the surface as foam forms. Reduce the heat to low, cover and simmer for 2½ hours or until nearly soft. **TWO** Meanwhile, coarsely slice 1½ onions and grate the remaining onion. If using canned chickpeas, bring the water to the boil and add with the grated onion, chicken, bouquet garni and saffron. Bring to the boil, then reduce the heat to low, cover and simmer for 10 minutes. **THREE** Add the sliced onions and raisins to the pan. Bring to the boil, then reduce the heat, cover and simmer for a further 20 minutes. Spoon a little of the stock into a bowl and stir in the turmeric until dissolved. Add to the pan and cook for a further 10 minutes or until the chicken is tender. **FOUR** Meanwhile, cover the couscous with water. Rake it through with your fingers, then drain and immediately spread it evenly over a large tray or shallow pan. Rake the grains with your fingers a few times to aerate them, then leave for 20–30 minutes until the water is absorbed and the couscous is relatively dry. **FIVE** Rub the couscous gently between your palms, allowing it to fall back into the tray or pan, to break down any lumps. **SIX** Measure 450 ml (¾ pint) of the stock into a pan, taste and adjust the seasonings and bring to a rapid boil. Remove the pan from the heat and quickly add the couscous, then cover and leave for 10 minutes or until the stock has been fully absorbed. **SEVEN** To serve, place the couscous in a circle on a serving plate and pile the chicken in the middle. Serve the remaining sauce alongside. Serve hot or warm.

Serves 4–6

NUTRIENT ANALYSIS PER SERVING 2099 kJ – 498 kcal – 49 g protein – 67 g carbohydrate – 18 g sugars – 6 g fat – 1 g saturates – 5 g fibre – 0.2 g sodium

recipe illustrated on pages 104–105

TAGINE OF CHICKEN AND OLIVES

INGREDIENTS 1 small–medium chicken, cut into 3–4 pieces │ 300 ml (½ pint) water │ 1 lemon sliced │ good pinch of saffron threads │ 4 garlic cloves, crushed │ pinch of salt │ 1 teaspoon extra virgin olive oil │ ½ teaspoon ground ginger │ ½ teaspoon paprika │ ¾ teaspoon ground cumin │ 200 g (7 oz) pitted green olives, rinsed │ 2 tablespoons lemon juice

ONE Put the chicken and water in a medium pan and bring slowly to the boil, skimming the surface as foam forms. Add the lemon, saffron, garlic, salt, oil and half the ginger. Reduce the heat to medium, cover and simmer for 50–60 minutes or until the chicken is tender. **TWO** Add the remaining ginger, the paprika and cumin and stir gently – try not to break up the chicken. Alternatively, remove the chicken and remove the bones, then return it to the sauce – you should have about 150 ml (¼ pint) or a little over. Add the olives and lemon juice, simmer for about 5 minutes, then serve hot.

Serves 4–5

NUTRIENT ANALYSIS PER SERVING 2025 kJ – 488 kcal – 41 g protein – 1 g carbohydrate – 0 g sugars – 36 g fat – 9 g saturates – 2 g fibre – 1.2 g sodium

HEALTHY TIP Olives are excellent food for the heart as they are naturally low in sodium. Nevertheless, they must be consumed in moderation since they're pickled in salt.

B'STEEYA WITH CHICKEN

While I was in Fez, Madame Sefraoui kindly explained the stages of this recipe to me.

INGREDIENTS 1 small–medium chicken, cut into 4 pieces │ 450 ml (¾ pint) water │ 2 large cinnamon sticks │ 750 g (1½ lb) onions, finely chopped │ 1½ teaspoons salt, or to taste │ good pinch of saffron threads │ 2 large handfuls finely chopped parsley │ 1 large handful finely chopped coriander leaves │ ¾–1 teaspoon ground ginger │ ¼ teaspoon black pepper │ ½ teaspoon turmeric │ 1½ tablespoons extra virgin olive oil, plus extra for greasing │ 4 eggs │ 250 g (8 oz) blanched almonds │ 1¼ tablespoons icing sugar, or to taste │ 1 heaped teaspoon ground cinnamon │ 7 sheets of filo pastry

ONE Bring the chicken and water slowly to the boil in a pan, skimming the surface as foam forms. Add the cinnamon sticks, onions and salt, cover and simmer until the onions have softened. Add the saffron and cook for 30 minutes. **TWO** Add the parsley, coriander, ginger, pepper, turmeric and 1 tablespoon of the oil, cover and simmer for 15–20 minutes until the chicken is tender. **THREE** Remove the chicken and cool slightly. Discard the skin and bones and cut the meat into bite-sized pieces. **FOUR** Set aside just under half the onion mixture. Beat 3 eggs and 1 egg white, add to the sauce in the pan and cook, stirring continuously, for 5 minutes or until thick. Let cool. **FIVE** Brown the almonds on a baking sheet in a preheated oven, 180°C (350°F) Gas Mark 4, for 10–15 minutes, then sprinkle with 1 teaspoon of the icing sugar and ¼ teaspoon of the cinnamon. Let cool, then chop coarsely. **SIX** Place a filo sheet horizontally across a greased 30 cm (12 inch) pan and another across vertically. Fold another sheet in half and place on top. Spread with the almonds. Fold another sheet in half and place over the almonds, then spread the egg sauce over this. Mix the chicken with the reserved sauce and spread over the egg. Sprinkle with the remaining cinnamon and 2 teaspoons icing sugar. Fold in the overhanging edges, cover with 2–3 more filo sheets and gently tuck these in underneath. Brush with the remaining oil and egg yolk, beaten. Bake in a preheated oven, 190°C (375°F) Gas Mark 5, for 30–40 minutes. **SEVEN** Sprinkle with the remaining icing sugar.

Serves 6–8

NUTRIENT ANALYSIS PER SERVING 3424 kJ – 824 kcal – 48 g protein – 37 g carbohydrate – 12 g sugars – 55 g fat – 10 g saturates – 8 g fibre – 0.8 g sodium (if using 1½ teaspoons salt)

recipe illustrated on pages 110–111

STEAMED CHICKEN STUFFED WITH AROMATIC RICE

This dish requires a bit of time to prepare, but it is not at all difficult and frankly I never bother to truss the chicken. In Morocco, a variety of stuffings are used – couscous with almonds and raisins, for instance. I love to stuff it with coarse bulgar wheat or with rice, as in this recipe.

INGREDIENTS 1 small–medium chicken │ finely chopped pitted black olives and finely chopped red peppers, to garnish │ salt and black pepper (optional)

STUFFING 175 g (6 oz) brown basmati rice, rinsed once and drained │ 2 tomatoes, skinned, deseeded and chopped │ 2 tablespoons finely chopped parsley │ 2 tablespoons finely chopped coriander leaves │ 1 heaped teaspoon finely chopped thyme │ ½ teaspoon turmeric │ ½ teaspoon ground cumin │ 1 teaspoon salt │ 1 tablespoon extra virgin olive oil │ 1 tablespoon lemon juice

ONE If you like, rub the chicken with a little salt and pepper. Thoroughly mix together all the ingredients for the stuffing and stuff the chicken at the neck end. Pull the neck flap over the stuffing to cover and, if you like, secure with a skewer. **TWO** Fill the bottom half of a couscoussière, or saucepan, a little over half full with water and bring to the boil. Put the chicken in the perforated top section, or in a steamer, and place over the boiling water. Cover and steam for 1½ hours. **THREE** Check the rice in the stuffing. If it's cooked, remove the pan, otherwise leave it for a little longer. **FOUR** Transfer the chicken to a hot dish. Mix the olives with the red peppers, garnish the chicken and serve.

Serves 4–6

NUTRIENT ANALYSIS PER SERVING 1570 kJ – 375 kcal – 19 g protein – 38 g carbohydrate – 3 g sugars – 17 g fat – 4g saturates – 3 g fibre – 0.9 g sodium

HEALTHY TIP This nutritious, one-pot meal is an excellent source of protein, indispensable for growth and immunity; it is rich in the B vitamins important for the nervous system; in iron, a deficiency of which creates fatigue; in zinc, which keeps the immune system in good shape; and in potassium, to regulate blood pressure.

recipe illustrated on pages 114–115

LAMB

LAMB TAGINE WITH PRUNES AND APRICOTS

This dish brings to mind the cultural, religious, medieval city of Fez, which I visited during their festival of culinary arts. While there, I tasted many delicious tagines, among them a speciality from the north with veal, apricots and walnuts, and another from the south with figs and walnuts. Despite its sweetness, I like to eat this tagine with baked sweet potato and plain couscous or bulgar wheat.

INGREDIENTS ½ tablespoon olive oil | handful of blanched almonds | 4 lamb shanks or 500 g (1 lb) boned lamb from the knuckle | 250 g (8 oz) onions, chopped | 1¼ teaspoons ground ginger | 30 coriander seeds, ground | ¼ teaspoon ground saffron | ¼ teaspoon black pepper | 1 teaspoon turmeric | ½ teaspoon salt | 1 large cinnamon stick | 200–300 ml (7 fl oz–½ pint) hot water | 12 prunes, soaked and drained | 2 slices of orange rind | ½ heaped teaspoon ground cinnamon | 1 tablespoon dark honey | 1 teaspoon clarified butter *(see page 18)* | 4 dried apricots, soaked and drained | pinch of freshly grated nutmeg | 1 tablespoon orange flower water | large handful of coriander leaves | 1 tablespoon toasted sesame seeds, to garnish

ONE Heat the pan, add the oil and sauté the almonds until golden. Add the lamb and onions and sauté until brown. Add the ginger, ground coriander, saffron, pepper, turmeric, salt and cinnamon stick, stir for a few seconds, then add the water and bring to the boil (the amount of water depends on the quality of the meat – the better the meat, the less water it will need). Reduce the heat to low, cover and simmer for 1 hour, or until the meat is very tender. **TWO** Add the prunes, orange rind and ground cinnamon and bring to the boil, then reduce the heat, cover and simmer for 15–20 minutes. **THREE** Add the honey, butter, apricots, nutmeg, flower water and coriander leaves, increase the heat and leave to bubble for about 10 minutes until caramelized, but do not allow it to dry out. **FOUR** Remove from the heat and leave for 5 minutes for the flavours to mellow (the sauce must be concentrated), then garnish with the sesame seeds and serve.

Serves 4

NUTRIENT ANALYSIS PER SERVING 1604 kJ – 383 kcal – 29 g protein – 22 g carbohydrate – 21 g sugars – 20 g fat – 8 g saturates – 6 g fibre – 0.4 g sodium

HEALTHY TIP Apricots are rich in betacarotene and lycopene (good for the eyes). Adding an apple would also be good, as it would counterbalance the saturated fatty acids of the meat and butter. The pectin in the apricots thickens the liquor, but most importantly, it slows the absorption of sugars into the bloodstream and gives a sense of satiety.

recipe illustrated on pages 122–123

KEFTA WITH AROMATIC HERBS

This dish makes an excellent meal eaten with **Tomato, Cucumber and Pepper salad** *(see page 58)* **or, for a variation, try adding the keftas to a quantity of Aromatic Tomato Sauce** *(see page 19)* **and simmering for 5 minutes.**

INGREDIENTS 65 g (2½ oz) onion | 65 g (2½ oz) parsley | 65 g (2½ oz) coriander leaves | 1 teaspoon ground cumin | 1 teaspoon paprika | heaped ¼ teaspoon cayenne pepper | 1 teaspoon salt | 500 g (1 lb) lean minced lamb

ONE Put all the ingredients except the meat in a food processor and whiz briefly. Add the meat and whiz again until mixed. Alternatively, grate the onion, chop the parsley and coriander finely and mix with the other ingredients. **TWO** Divide the mixture into 18–24 pieces and roll each into a ball. Mould each ball around a skewer, pressing the meat gently yet firmly into a sausage shape. **THREE** Place the keftas under a preheated hot grill and cook for 3–5 minutes on each side until browned.

Serves 4

NUTRIENT ANALYSIS PER SERVING 923 kJ – 220 kcal – 27 g protein – 2 g carbohydrate – 2 g sugars – 12 g fat – 5 g saturates – 2 g fibre – 0.6 g sodium

HEALTHY TIP This is rich in the building blocks of protein, iron, carotene, vitamin C, phosphorus, zinc and potassium.

LAMB AND ARTICHOKE TAGINE

Moroccans are fond of artichoke tagine, which has a delicate and tasty flavour. This recipe was given to me during my stay in Rabat, the capital of Morocco. Fresh artichokes do take a little time to prepare, but they are worth it for their flavour.

INGREDIENTS 500 g (1 lb) boned lamb (leg or shoulder), cut into medium-sized pieces | 600 ml (1 pint) water | 1 teaspoon salt, or to taste | 1 bay leaf | 1 cinnamon stick | 200 g (7 oz) onions, sliced | 3 large garlic cloves, crushed | good pinch of saffron threads | ¾ tablespoon extra virgin olive oil | 4 fresh artichokes or canned artichoke hearts | lemon juice | ¼ teaspoon black pepper | good pinch of freshly grated root ginger | 25 g (1 oz) finely chopped parsley | 25 g (1 oz) finely chopped coriander leaves | 450 ml (¾ pint) water | I teaspoon salt, or to taste | ½ teaspoon turmeric | 200 g (7 oz) basmati rice, rinsed once and drained | 1 teaspoon extra virgin olive oil

ONE Put the lamb and water in a medium pan and bring slowly to the boil, skimming the surface as foam forms. Add the salt, bay leaf, cinnamon stick, onions, garlic, saffron and oil and return to the boil. Reduce the heat, cover and simmer for 40 minutes. **TWO** Meanwhile, if using fresh artichokes, remove all the leaves (save these to steam later). Using a pointed knife, remove and discard the choke from the centre of each artichoke. Trim the heart, rinse with cold water and rub with lemon juice to prevent discoloration. **THREE** At the end of cooking time for the meat, drain the canned artichokes, if using, slice each fresh or canned artichoke heart into quarters and add to the pan. Bring to the boil, then reduce the heat, cover and cook for a further 15–20 minutes or until the meat is tender. About 5 minutes before the end of cooking time season with the pepper and fresh ginger and add the parsley and coriander. **FOUR** Meanwhile, cook the rice. Bring the water and salt to the boil, add the turmeric and the rice. Reduce the heat to low, cover and simmer for 6–7 minutes or until the water has been absorbed and the rice is cooked. A couple of minutes before the rice is ready, gently stir in the oil with a fork. **FIVE** Serve the tagine with the rice.

Serves 4

NUTRIENT ANALYSIS PER SERVING 1958 kJ – 468 kcal – 33 g protein – 50 g carbohydrate – 3 g sugars – 15 g fat – 6 g saturates – 1 g fibre – 1 g sodium (if using 1¾ teaspoons salt)

HEALTHY TIP Artichokes are low in calories, diuretic and they eliminate toxins and are ideal for diabetics. This dish is also valuable in B and C vitamins, potassium, iron, calcium, phosphorus and magnesium.

recipe illustrated on pages 128–129

HONEYED LAMB TAGINE

This tagine (*Mrouzia*) is the traditional Moroccan dish cooked for *Id el-Kabir* (big feast), the festival of the sacrifice of Abraham, during which it is customary to distribute meat to the poor. It has an amazing balance of flavours and makes a great lunch or dinner. It is enjoyable and quite therapeutic to prepare. The neck, shoulder or leg of lamb are all excellent to use and for a richer flavour, add a lamb bone.

INGREDIENTS ½ tablespoon Ras al-hanout *(see page 16)* │ ½ teaspoon ground ginger │ pinch of black pepper │ ¼ teaspoon ground saffron │ ½ teaspoon ground cinnamon │ 500 g (1 lb) boned lamb (neck, leg or shoulder), cut into medium–large chunks │ 125 g (4 oz) raisins │ 1–2 tablespoons extra virgin olive oil │ 1 onion, about 225 g (7½ oz), finely chopped │ 65 g (2½ oz) blanched almonds │ 1 large cinnamon stick │ 1 bay leaf │ ½ teaspoon salt │ 300 ml (½ pint) hot water, or as necessary │ 1 heaped tablespoon dark honey │ 1 teaspoon turmeric (optional)

ONE Put the Ras al-hanout in a small bowl, add the ginger, pepper, saffron, cinnamon and about a tablespoon of water and mix thoroughly. Rub three-quarters of this spice mixture into the meat, coating it on all sides. Mix the remainder in with the raisins. **TWO** Heat the oil in a pan, then add the meat, onion, almonds, cinnamon stick and bay leaf and sprinkle with the salt. Stir together, then cook for 5–7 minutes, stirring occasionally. **THREE** Add the hot water, cover and simmer over a medium heat for about 1 hour or until the meat is very tender, stirring occasionally and checking the water – if necessary top up with more hot water. **FOUR** When the meat is tender and the liquid has reduced, add the raisins, honey and turmeric, if using, and cook for a further 5–8 minutes, stirring from time to time to prevent the ingredients from sticking to the pan. **FIVE** Serve hot with roasted or baked sweet potatoes, or couscous and Grated Carrot and Orange Salad *(see page 48)*.

Serves 3–4

NUTRIENT ANALYSIS PER SERVING 2720 kJ – 650 kcal – 40 g protein – 47 g carbohydrate – 44 g sugars – 35 g fat – 9 g saturates – 7 g fibre – 0.5 g sodium

recipe illustrated on pages 132–133

LAMB WITH DATES AND HONEY

What an unusual mixture! The meat simmers gently with potent herbs, to which are added the powerful flavours of saffron and cinnamon and the natural sugars of honey and dates. From this amazing blend emerges an excellent velvety texture and soothing taste. All you need are good quality ingredients and love while cooking it. With these salées-sucrées dishes, I like to serve sweet potato, rich in carotene and an Orange and Olive Salad *(see page 75).*

INGREDIENTS 1 tablespoon extra virgin olive oil | handful of flaked almonds | 500 g (1 lb) boned lamb (leg or shoulder), cut into 4 pieces | 200–300 ml (7 fl oz–½ pint) water | 160 g (5½ oz) onions, finely chopped | 25 g (1 oz) chopped coriander leaves | 1 large garlic clove, crushed | a few fennel slices, about 125 g (4 oz) | ½–1 teaspoon salt | ½ teaspoon saffron threads | 1 teaspoon ground cinnamon | pinch or ½ teaspoon sugar | 1 heaped tablespoon dark honey | 8 dates (preferably medjool), stoned

ONE Heat the oil gently in a medium pan and sauté the almonds, stirring continuously, until golden but not too browned. Alternatively, put the almonds on a baking sheet and toast in a preheated oven, 180°C (350°F) Gas Mark 4, for about 10 minutes. Remove and put to one side.

TWO Add the lamb to the pan and brown all over on a medium-high heat for about 5 minutes. Add 200 ml (7 fl oz) of the water and bring slowly to the boil, skimming the surface as foam forms. Add the onions, coriander, garlic, fennel, salt and saffron. Return to the boil, then reduce the heat to low, cover and simmer for about 50 minutes or until the meat is tender.

THREE Check the amount of sauce – there should be enough to serve 2–3 tablespoons with each portion. If not, add the extra hot water. Sprinkle with the cinnamon, sugar and honey and stir well. Bring to the boil, then reduce the heat and simmer for 5 minutes. **FOUR** Add the dates, simmer for 8–10 minutes until the sauce is moderately thick, then remove from the heat and leave for 5 minutes before serving.

Serves 4

NUTRIENT ANALYSIS PER SERVING 1566 kJ – 374 kcal – 28 g protein – 30 g carbohydrate – 12 g sugars – 16 g fat – 6 g saturates – 1 g fibre – 0.4 g sodium

HEALTHY TIP This dish is energy giving, a diuretic and calming, very rich in protein, B vitamins, fibre, potassium, magnesium, zinc, calcium and phosphates.

TAGINE OF LAMB AND GREEN BEANS

While I was in Fez, my guide Hisham took me to a beautifully ornate restaurant where I ate this tagine, which has more sauce than other tagines. Its flavours travelled back with me to London and I prepared it straight away. This dish is succulent and wholesome and so comforting and satisfying that you will want to have more helpings. Serve fresh fruit such as apples, pears or oranges to finish the meal.

INGREDIENTS 500 g (1 lb) boned leg of lamb, cut into 8 pieces | 1¼ teaspoons salt, or to taste | 150 ml (¼ pint) water | 1 tablespoon thick extra virgin olive oil | 40 g (1½ oz) onion | good pinch of saffron threads | ½ teaspoon ground ginger | ½ teaspoon paprika | 4 tomatoes, skinned, deseeded and chopped | 1.1 kg (1 lb 2 oz) green beans | 1 heaped teaspoon double-concentrated tomato purée | ¾ teaspoon turmeric | 1½ tablespoons lemon juice

ONE Place the lamb in a small–medium pan, sprinkle with the salt and rub in, then leave for 5 minutes. **TWO** Put the pan over a medium heat, and when the meat juices start to appear, add the water, oil, onion and half the saffron, ginger and paprika. Stir for 1–2 minutes, then stir in the tomatoes and top with the beans. Reduce the heat to low, cover the pan and simmer for 1 hour or until the meat is tender. Check the water level from time to time and if necessary add a little hot water. **THREE** About 15 minutes before the end of cooking time add the tomato purée. A few minutes before the end of cooking time add the remaining saffron, ginger and paprika and the turmeric, cover and simmer to finish cooking. **FOUR** Add the lemon juice, shake the pan and remove from the heat. Leave for a few minutes to allow the flavours to come together, then serve hot with bread.

Serves 3–4

NUTRIENT ANALYSIS PER SERVING 1782 kJ – 427 kcal – 43 g protein – 19 g carbohydrate – 15 g sugars – 21 g fat – 8 g saturates – 13 g fibre – 1 g sodium (if using 1¼ teaspoons salt)

HEALTHY TIP We should avoid eating sauces that are rich in saturated fats, so in this dish no butter is used and the meat is extra lean. It's a great source of the potent anti-cancerous lycopene and other protective nutrients such as A and B vitamins, potassium, phosphorus, zinc and magnesium – all important for the functioning of enzymes, which augment the ability of intellect and prevent stress. This is good for growing children, very active people and also diabetics.

recipe illustrated on pages 138–139

TAGINE OF LAMB WITH PUMPKIN

Here is another delicious way of preparing lamb, and a perfect meal for the cold winter. The flavour of the meat and spices marry well with the delicacy of the pumpkin. The dish can be prepared ahead of time and reheated as needed.

INGREDIENTS 500 g (1 lb) boned lamb (leg or shoulder), cut into medium-sized pieces | 1 tablespoon extra virgin olive oil | 1 small onion, studded with 1 clove | 350 ml (12 fl oz) water | 2 garlic cloves, crushed | 1 bay leaf | 1 cinnamon stick | pinch of saffron threads | 1½ teaspoons salt, or to taste | ½ teaspoon ground ginger | 1.1 kg (2 lb 2 oz) peeled pumpkin, deseeded and cubed | 1 teaspoon sugar | 1 teaspoon dark honey | ¾ teaspoon turmeric

ONE Heat a pan, then add the lamb, 1 teaspoon of the oil and the onion. Stir for a few seconds, then add the water and bring slowly to the boil, skimming the surface as foam forms. Reduce the heat to low, add the garlic, bay leaf, cinnamon stick, saffron and 1 teaspoon of the salt and simmer for 1 hour or until the meat is very tender. Five minutes before the end of cooking time, dissolve the ginger in a little of the lamb stock and add to the pan. **TWO** Meanwhile, put the pumpkin in a large shallow pan, stir in the remaining salt and heat gently. As the pumpkin softens, break it down with the back of a wooden spoon and stir occasionally until the water evaporates. **THREE** Stir in the remaining oil, sprinkle with the sugar and honey and cook for 8 minutes, or until the pumpkin caramelizes. Dissolve the turmeric in a little of the lamb stock and stir into the pumpkin, cook for few more seconds then taste and adjust the seasonings. **FOUR** To serve, place the pumpkin purée on a hot serving dish and top with the meat and sauce.

Serves 4

NUTRIENT ANALYSIS PER SERVING 1163 kJ – 278 kcal – 28 g protein – 10 g carbohydrate – 8 g sugars – 14 g fat – 6 g saturates – 2 g fibre – 0.8 g sodium (if using 1½ teaspoons salt)

HEALTHY TIP This dish has a good quality of protein and is very rich in minerals such as iron (necessary to produce energy) and zinc, and in fibre.

LAMB STUFFED WITH COUSCOUS

Although the stuffing needs care and the cooking is long and slow, this is a delicious and special dish for entertaining friends or family.

INGREDIENTS 500 g (1 lb) organic couscous │ ½ teaspoon salt │ ½ tablespoon orange flower water │ 50 g (2 oz) flaked almonds │ 25 g (1 oz) raisins │ pinch of freshly grated nutmeg │ 1½ teaspoons ground cinnamon │ ½ tablespoon extra virgin olive oil │ 2.25 kg (5 lb) shoulder of lamb, boned │ 1.2 litres (2 pints) water │ a few saffron threads │ bouquet garni: 1 large cinnamon stick, 1 onion studded with 2 cloves, 2 bay leaves, 1 celery stick │ good pinch of black pepper │ 1 tablespoon dark honey │ 1 teaspoon fructose (fruit sugar)

ONE Rinse 175 g (6 oz) of the couscous, rake it through with your fingers, then drain and immediately spread it evenly over a large tray or shallow pan. Rake the grains with your fingers a few times to aerate them, then leave for 20–30 minutes until the water is absorbed and the couscous is relatively dry. **TWO** Sprinkle the salt, 4 tablespoons of water, the flower water and almonds over the couscous, rake with your fingers a few times to aerate the grains and leave to absorb the liquid. When dry, rub the grains gently between your palms, allowing it to fall back into the tray or pan, to break down any lumps. Add the raisins, nutmeg, ½ teaspoon of the cinnamon and the oil. **THREE** Stuff the bone cavity of the lamb with the couscous mixture and sew or secure to enclose the filling. Put the lamb in a large pan, add the water and bring slowly to the boil, skimming the surface as foam forms. Add the saffron and bouquet garni, reduce the heat to low and simmer for 2 hours. Turn the meat over and simmer for 1–2 hours or until very tender. To reduce the saturated fat content, remove from the heat and cool, then chill the lamb and stock separately. The next day, remove the solidified fat, reheat the lamb in the stock and continue as below. **FOUR** Remove the onion, discard the cloves and press the onion through a sieve over the pan. Sprinkle with the pepper, the remaining cinnamon, the honey and fructose, increase the heat and cook for 15 minutes until caramelized, but do not let it dry out. **FIVE** Ladle 450 ml (I pint) of the stock into a small pan, bring to the boil and add the remaining couscous. Turn off the heat, cover and leave for 10 minutes to absorb the stock. Taste, adjust the seasonings and serve with the lamb.

Serves 6–8

NUTRIENT ANALYSIS PER SERVING 4108 kJ – 988 kcal – 60 g protein – 52 g carbohydrate – 9 g sugars – 61 g fat – 26 g saturates – 1 g fibre – 0.4 g sodium

LEMONY LAMB AND RICE

INGREDIENTS 500 g (1 lb) boned leg of lamb, cut into medium chunks │ 1½ teaspoons salt │ 600 ml (1 pint) water │ pinch of saffron threads │ 125 g (4 oz) onions, grated │ 1 lemon quarter │ ½ tablespoon ground almonds │ 2 tablespoons chopped parsley │ 1 tablespoon chopped coriander leaves │ 1 tomato, skinned, deseeded and chopped │ ½ tablespoon lemon juice │ pinch of black pepper │ 200 g (7 oz) basmati rice, rinsed and drained

ONE Sprinkle the lamb with 1 teaspoon salt, place in a pan and leave for a few minutes. Add the water and bring slowly to the boil, skimming as foam forms. Add the saffron, onions and lemon and return to the boil. Reduce the heat to low, cover and simmer for 1 hour or until the meat is tender. 15 minutes before the end of cooking add the almonds, parsley, coriander and tomato. A few minutes later stir in the lemon juice and pepper. **TWO** Ladle out 450 ml (¾ pint) of the stock into a small pan and add the rice and remaining salt. Bring to the boil, then reduce the heat to low, cover and simmer for 8 minutes or until the stock is fully absorbed. **THREE** Transfer the rice to a serving dish and serve with the meat.

Serves 4–6

NUTRIENT ANALYSIS PER SERVING 1764 kJ – 420 kcal – 30 g protein – 43 g carbohydrate – 3 g sugars – 14 g fat – 5 g saturates – 1 g fibre – 0.9 g sodium (if using 1½ teaspoons salt)

SHREDS OF LAMB IN POMEGRANATE JUICE

This dish will delight meat lovers with its rich flavour and speedy preparation. In Arabic it's known as *Shahm* (fat), because lamb in the Middle East usually has a tail full of fat that melts easily, although this is not the case in Europe. My deviation from Ibn Razin el-Tujibi's 13th century recipe is to cut down on the saturated fat, which increases the risks of colon cancer. The recipe is said to be prepared in the north of Morocco, particularly in Tetouan. I have added the juice of a whole sour pomegranate, following the option he gave in the book. I have also added pomegranate syrup, which is left to one's choice. Accompany this dish with **Three Pepper Salad** *(see page 70).*

INGREDIENTS 750 g (1½ lb) boned lamb (leg or shoulder), cut into thin short strips | 1 teaspoon salt, or to taste | 1½ tablespoons extra virgin olive oil | ½ teaspoon black pepper | ½–¾ teaspoon ground caraway | ½–¾ teaspoon ground coriander | 1 tablespoon chopped coriander leaves | juice of 1 sour pomegranate, if available | 1 teaspoon lemon juice, if necessary | ½ tablespoon pomegranate syrup (optional)

ONE Put the meat in a shallow nonstick frying pan, season with the salt and cook over a medium-low heat for 1 minute. Add the oil and continue cooking, stirring occasionally, for about 8 minutes, or until thoroughly browned. Cover and leave to simmer for about 20 minutes, stirring from time to time, or until the liquid has evaporated. Taste a piece to check if it's done. Since the meat is thinly sliced, if it is of good quality it does not need water to tenderize it. **TWO** When the meat is tender, season with the pepper, caraway and the ground and fresh coriander, then stir well and cook for 1–2 minutes until the meat has browned and is nearly dry. Add the pomegranate juice, if using, and the lemon juice (if the pomegranate is not sour enough) and stir until the juices are absorbed by the meat. Taste and stir in the pomegranate syrup, if using. **THREE** Serve immediately with roast potatoes or fries and salads.

Serves 3–4

NUTRIENT ANALYSIS PER SERVING 2008 kJ – 480 kcal – 53 g protein – 2 g carbohydrate – 2 g sugars – 29 g fat – 12 g saturates – 3 g fibre – 0.9 g sodium (if using 1 teaspoon salt)

HEALTHY TIP This dish is an excellent source of protein, B vitamins, iron, phosphorus, potassium and zinc.

LAMB WITH TOMATOES AND ONIONS

What a glorious tagine! It is known in Morocco as *Maqfoul*, meaning 'locked'. My knowledgeable guide Siddik told me that a good tagine needs to simmer on the hob for at least 2½ hours – the slower, the tastier. Following this advice, towards the end of the simmering I sprinkled the dish lightly with icing sugar and finished its cooking in the oven.

INGREDIENTS 750 g (1½ lb) boned lamb (leg or shoulder), cut into medium-sized pieces │ 1 teaspoon salt, or to taste │ 125 ml (4 fl oz) water │ pinch of saffron threads │ 3 garlic cloves, crushed │ ½ teaspoon ground cinnamon │ 575 g (1 lb 3 oz) onions, each cut into quarters │ 1¼ tablespoons extra virgin olive oil │ about 1.1 kg (2 lb 2 oz) tomatoes, skinned, cut horizontally and deseeded │ ½ teaspoon turmeric │ pinch of freshly grated root ginger │ good pinch of black pepper │ 1 teaspoon icing sugar (optional)

ONE Pack the meat tightly in a single layer in a medium ovenproof pan. Sprinkle all over with the salt and leave to stand for 5 minutes. Add the water and bring slowly to the boil, skimming the surface as foam forms, then add the saffron, garlic, half the cinnamon and the onions, spreading them evenly over the meat. Drizzle all over with half the oil, then cover and simmer over a very low heat for 30 minutes. If necessary, place a heat diffuser under the pan. **TWO** Put half the tomatoes, cut side down, over the onions. Cover and simmer over a low heat for 1 hour. **THREE** Check the amount of liquid in the pan and if necessary pour some off, then add the turmeric, ginger and pepper. Gently shake the pan to distribute the spices evenly, then sprinkle all over with the remaining cinnamon and oil and the icing sugar, if using. Cover again and transfer to a preheated oven, 180°C (350°F) Gas Mark 4, for 20–30 minutes. Uncover the pan and cook for a further 5 minutes, then remove from the oven and serve.

Serves 4–5

NUTRIENT ANALYSIS PER SERVING 1847 kJ – 440 kcal – 43 g protein – 21 g carbohydrate – 18 g sugars – 21 g fat – 9 g saturates – 6 g fibre – 0.7 g sodium (if using 1 teaspoon salt)

HEALTHY TIP *Maqfoul* has valuable nutrients that oppose the free radicals that destroy healthy cells. It supplies A and B vitamins, phosphorus, magnesium, potassium, iron, zinc, quercetin, selenium and sulphur.

TAGINE OF LAMB AND AUBERGINE

During my stay in Fez, Madame Sefraoui suggested this dish. It was so delicious that I couldn't wait to prepare it at home. Rather than frying the aubergines, you can slice them into rounds, brush with oil and grill to brown on both sides.

INGREDIENTS 625 g (1¼ lb) aubergines, sliced lengthways into 1.5 cm (¾ inch) widths │ salt │ 500 g (1 lb) boned lamb (shoulder or leg), cut into 4–8 equal pieces │ extra virgin olive oil, as necessary │ pinch of saffron threads │ ½ teaspoon ground ginger │ ¼ teaspoon ground coriander │ 150 ml (¼ pint) water │ 1 kg (2 lb) tomatoes, skinned, deseeded and coarsely chopped │ 2 garlic cloves, finely crushed │ I teaspoon paprika │ ½ teaspoon turmeric │ ¾ teaspoon ground cumin │ 1 tablespoon finely chopped coriander leaves │ 1 tablespoon finely chopped parsley │ ½ teaspoon sugar │ ¾–1 tablespoon lemon juice │ crusty bread, to serve (optional)

ONE If the aubergines are very large, salt the slices all over, place in a sieve over a bowl and leave for 1–2 hours to drain. **TWO** Meanwhile, rub the lamb with ½ teaspoon of salt and place in a small–medium pan and leave for 5 minutes. Add ½ teaspoon of oil to the meat, place over a medium heat and stir for about 1 minute, then add the saffron, ginger and ground coriander and stir well. Add 50 ml (2 fl oz) of the water, reduce the heat to very low, cover and simmer for about 1 hour or until the meat is very tender. Check the water level from time to time – you may need to add another 3–4 tablespoons of hot water. **THREE** Meanwhile, put the tomatoes, garlic and a pinch of salt in a small frying pan, place over a medium heat and simmer for 1–2 minutes, then add the paprika. Continue cooking until nearly all the water has evaporated, then stir in the turmeric, cumin, 1 teaspoon of oil, fresh coriander, parsley and sugar and cook until it reaches a thick consistency. **FOUR** Rinse the aubergines very well, gently squeeze out the excess water and dry the slices between kitchen paper. Heat some oil until hot but not smoking, then fry the aubergine slices on both sides until brown. Remove and drain well on several changes of kitchen paper. Leave to cool to room temperature, then drizzle with lemon juice and, using a fork, mash to mix them thoroughly with the juice. **FIVE** Place the mashed aubergines on the meat, top with the tomato mixture, cover and simmer for 10 minutes. **SIX** Shake the pan, but do not stir. Serve with bread, if using.

Serves 4–5

NUTRIENT ANALYSIS PER SERVING 1252 kJ – 298 kcal – 29 g protein – 12 g carbohydrate – 12 g sugars – 15 g fat – 6 g saturates – 7 g fibre – 0.4 g sodium

recipe illustrated on pages 152–153

TAGINE OF LAMB, QUINCE AND HONEY

Here is a delicious dish. The marriage of fruits, meat and spices is sensual and exciting to work with, mouth-watering and addictive. The spices produce a wonderful aroma, while the quinces have substances that help break down the fat and meat.

INGREDIENTS ½ tablespoon extra virgin olive oil │ 500 g (1 lb) boned lamb (leg or shoulder), cut into medium-sized pieces, fat trimmed │ 450 ml (¾ pint) water │ ½ teaspoon salt │ ¼ teaspoon black pepper │ ½ teaspoon saffron threads │ 2 cinnamon sticks │ 1 bay leaf │ 2 cloves │ 1 celery stick, cut into 3 pieces │ 1–2 quinces, unpeeled, each cut into 4 pieces and deseeded │ 1 teaspoon brown sugar │ ¾ teaspoon cinnamon │ ½ tablespoon dark honey

ONE Heat the pan, then add the oil and the lamb and sauté over a medium-high heat for a few minutes to brown the meat on all sides. Add the water and bring slowly to the boil, skimming the surface as foam forms. Season with the salt, pepper and saffron and add the cinnamon sticks, bay leaf, cloves and celery. Return to the boil, then reduce the heat to medium-low, cover and simmer for 30 minutes. **TWO** Add the quince pieces and return to the boil, then reduce the heat, cover and cook for 30 minutes or until the meat and quinces are tender. At this stage, if wished, the quinces can be carefully removed from the pan and placed under a hot grill to brown, then returned to the pan to finish cooking. **THREE** Sprinkle with the sugar, cinnamon and honey and cook for a further 10–15 minutes. Taste, adjust the seasonings and serve with couscous or bulgar wheat.

Serves 4

NUTRIENT ANALYSIS PER SERVING 1017 kJ – 242 kcal – 26 g protein – 7 g carbohydrate – 7 g sugars – 13 g fat – 6 g saturates – 2 g fibre – 0.4 g sodium

HEALTHY TIP This dish is rich in protein, iron, zinc, B vitamins and fibre.

FISH

FISH IN AROMATIC SAUCE

INGREDIENTS 1.1 kg (2 lb 2 oz) sea bass or hake, gutted and scaled │ 1 teaspoon salt, or to taste │ 500 g (1 lb) potatoes, thinly sliced │ 500 g (1 lb) tomatoes, each cut into 3 │ 1 quantity Chermoula Sauce *(see page 14)* │ 1 green or red pepper, cored, deseeded and cut into 2–3 slices │ 2 whole chillies │ 3 tablespoons extra virgin olive oil

ONE Wash the fish with cold water and pat dry. Sprinkle inside and out with ½ teaspoon of the salt. Mix the potatoes and tomatoes with the remaining salt and about 1 tablespoon of the Chermoula Sauce. **TWO** Make a bed of potatoes in a baking tray. Smear the fish inside and outside with the remaining Chermoula Sauce and place it on top of the potatoes. **THREE** Arrange the tomatoes, sliced peppers and chillies around and on top of the fish. Drizzle with the oil and bake in a preheated oven, 180°C (350°F) Gas Mark 4, for 30–40 minutes, basting twice. Remove from the oven and serve.

Serves 4

NUTRIENT ANALYSIS PER SERVING 1925 kJ – 460 kcal – 41 g protein – 82 g carbohydrate – 5 g sugars – 20 g fat – 2 g saturates – 4 g fibre – 1.1 g sodium (if using 1 teaspoon salt)

B'STEEYA OF FISH

I got this recipe during my stay in Essaouira, on the Atlantic coast, which was a Phoenician staging post in earlier times. It is easy to prepare and will appeal even to children who do not like fish.

INGREDIENTS 1.1 kg (2 lb 2 oz) sea bass, gutted and scaled | 1½ teaspoons ground cumin | pinch of salt | 1 tablespoon extra virgin olive oil | 3 sheets of filo pastry | 1 egg yolk

RICE 150 g (5 oz) basmati rice, rinsed once and drained | 300 ml (½ pint) water | ½ teaspoon salt | 2 tablespoons extra virgin olive oil | 5–6 heaped tablespoons chopped coriander leaves

ONE Steam the fish over boiling water for 8–10 minutes, or brush with oil and bake in a preheated oven, 180°C (350°F) Gas Mark 4, for 18–20 minutes. Remove, and when cool enough to handle, discard the skin and bones. Put the fish in a bowl, sprinkle with the cumin, salt and ½ tablespoon of the oil and mix thoroughly. Divide into 4 equal portions. **TWO** Put the rice, water and salt in a heavy-based pan. Bring to the boil, then reduce the heat to low, cover and simmer for 6–8 minutes or until the water has been absorbed. Add the oil and stir to mix with the rice, then add the coriander and mix thoroughly. Divide the rice into 4 equal portions. **THREE** Take 2 sheets of filo pastry and fold in half. Slice to get 4 equal sheets and place under a clean damp tea towel. Fold the remaining sheet once and fold again and again until you end up with a square shape. Using a 12 cm (5 inch) diameter plate as a template, and a pointed knife, slice around the plate to get neat filo rounds. **FOUR** To assemble, take one of the larger pastry sheets and place a smaller round in the middle, to strengthen the base. Spoon on a portion of rice and press lightly to form a circular shape. Place another pastry round on top of the rice. Spoon a portion of fish on to the round and press lightly as before. Brush the overhanging edges of the pastry with egg yolk and fold over the filling to form a round. Brush all over with a little of the remaining oil and egg yolk. Repeat with the remaining ingredients to make 4 pies. **FIVE** Bake on a lower shelf in a preheated oven, 190°C (375°F) Gas Mark 5, for 10–15 minutes or until golden brown.

Serves 4

NUTRIENT ANALYSIS PER SERVING 1970 kJ – 470 kcal – 40 g protein – 44 g carbohydrate – 1 g sugars – 15 g fat – 2 g saturates – 0 g fibre – 0.5 g sodium

recipe illustrated on pages 164–165

SARDINES IN AROMATIC HERBS

INGREDIENTS 300 g (10 oz) sardine fillets │ 2 large garlic cloves, crushed │ 1 small slice of onion, grated │ 25 g (1 oz) coriander leaves │ 1¼ teaspoons ground cumin │ scant ½ teaspoon black pepper │ ½ teaspoon turmeric │ 1¼ teaspoons salt, or to taste │ 1 tablespoon extra virgin olive oil │ 175 g (6 oz) onions, sliced │ a few saffron threads │ ¾ tablespoon tomato purée │ 2 large tomatoes, skinned, deseeded and finely chopped │ ½ red pepper, cored, deseeded and sliced into thin strips │ 150 ml (¼ pint) water │ handful of finely chopped parsley │ handful of finely chopped coriander leaves │ 2–3 small chillies, halved and deseeded │ handful of fresh or frozen peas │ 1½ tablespoons lemon juice, or to taste

ONE Put the sardines, garlic, grated onion, coriander, ¾ teaspoon of the cumin, the pepper, ¼ teaspoon of the turmeric and ¾ teaspoon of the salt in a food processor and whiz until smooth. Turn the mixture into a bowl and, working with moist hands, form into 16 balls slightly smaller than walnuts. Put to one side. **TWO** Heat a pan, add the oil and, when hot, add the sliced onions and sauté until translucent and yellowish in colour. Add the saffron, tomato purée, tomatoes, red pepper and water and bring to the boil, then reduce the heat to medium-low and simmer for a few minutes. **THREE** Add the sardine balls to the pan, sprinkle with the parsley and coriander, then add the chillies, peas and the remaining cumin, turmeric and salt. Cover and simmer for 8–10 minutes. **FOUR** Sprinkle with lemon juice and adjust the seasonings, then serve with barley semolina, couscous or rice.

Serves 3–4

NUTRIENT ANALYSIS PER SERVING 1125 kJ – 269 kcal – 24 g protein – 13 g carbohydrate – 10 g sugars – 14 g fat – 3 g saturates – 4 g fibre – 1 g sodium

HEALTHY TIP Sardines are an excellent source of omega-3 oils, which increase good cholesterol (HDL) in the body, reduce cardiovascular disease, boost immunity to prevent many cancers and nourish and rejuvenate cells in the brain and body. The fish are also high in zinc, which protects from prostate cancer. This is a nutritious dish rich in vitamin D, in lycopene antioxidant, in germanium, sulphur, selenium and co-enzyme Q-10, which is said to combat obesity, diabetes and much more.

recipe illustrated on pages 168–169

PRAWNS M'CHERMEL IN TOMATO SAUCE

INGREDIENTS 2 tablespoons finely chopped coriander leaves | 1 tablespoon finely chopped parsley | 2 garlic cloves | pinch of paprika | pinch of ground cumin | 1 teaspoon salt, or to taste | 1 tablespoon extra virgin olive oil | ½–1 tablespoon lemon juice | 16 large raw prawns, peeled | 125 g (4 oz) onions, finely chopped | ¼–½ teaspoon turmeric | 750 g (1½ lb) tomatoes, skinned, deseeded and chopped

ONE Put the coriander, parsley, garlic, paprika, cumin and ½ teaspoon of the salt in a mortar and pound with a pestle until creamy. Gradually add ½ tablespoon of the oil and ½ tablespoon of the lemon juice. Rub this sauce into the prawns, cover and refrigerate for at least 1 hour. **TWO** About 30 minutes before serving prepare the tomato sauce. Heat a frying pan and add the remaining oil, the onions, turmeric and tomatoes, sprinkle with the remaining salt and simmer over a medium-low heat for about 8 minutes. **THREE** Add the prawns and cook for about 4 minutes, until they turn pink in colour. Taste, add the remaining lemon juice if necessary and serve hot.

Serves 4

NUTRIENT ANALYSIS PER SERVING 454 kJ – 108 kcal – 9 g protein – 9 g carbohydrate – 8 g sugars – 4 g fat – 1 g saturates – 3 g fibre – 1 g sodium (if using 1 teaspoon salt)

FISH WITH PUMPKIN AND AROMATIC HERBS

This fish dish is prepared with carrots, pumpkin, olives and aromatic herbs – an astonishing combination maybe, but it still works extremely well and is delectable. The pumpkin and carrots are not pre-cooked, but, if desired, steaming or sautéeing them for a short while before adding to the stuffing cuts down on the baking time. Marinate the fish in the morning and cook it in the evening for a better flavour.

INGREDIENTS 1.1 kg (2 lb 2 oz) sea bass with head, gutted and scaled | 1½ teaspoons salt | 125 g (4 oz) peeled pumpkin, deseeded and coarsely grated | 125 g (4 oz) carrots, coarsely grated | 2 garlic cloves, crushed | about ½ teaspoon freshly grated root ginger | ¼ teaspoon black pepper | 12 black olives, pitted, rinsed and coarsely chopped | ½ teaspoon turmeric | ½ teaspoon cumin | 2 tablespoons finely chopped coriander leaves | 1 heaped tablespoon finely chopped parsley | ¼–½ teaspoon paprika | 1 teaspoon organic apple cider vinegar | 2–3 tablespoons extra virgin olive oil | 1 slice of preserved lemon *(see page 17)*, rinsed, pulp discarded and rind cut into small pieces (optional) | 2 tablespoons lemon juice

ONE Wash the fish with cold water, pat dry and score 2 diagonal cuts on each side. Rub the fish inside and out with ½ teaspoon of the salt. **TWO** Put the pumpkin and carrots in a bowl, add the garlic, the remaining salt, ginger, pepper, olives, turmeric, cumin, coriander, parsley, paprika, vinegar, 1½ tablespoons of the oil, the preserved lemon rind, if using, and lemon juice and mix thoroughly. **THREE** Stuff the fish cavity with the mixture, spread the remainder over the fish and put in a roasting tin. Drizzle with the remaining oil, ensuring that it is coated on all sides so that the fish does not stick to the tin. Cover and refrigerate for at least 1–2 hours to allow the fish to absorb the seasonings. **FOUR** Bake the fish in a preheated oven, 180°C (350°F) Gas Mark 4, for 30–40 minutes.

Serves 4

NUTRIENT ANALYSIS PER SERVING 1106 kJ – 264 kcal – 35 g protein – 4 g carbohydrate – 3 g sugars – 12 g fat – 2 g saturates – 2 g fibre – 1.3 g sodium

HEALTHY TIP A dish that's highly valuable as an excellent source of protein, betacarotene, vitamin C and selenium.

FISH TAGINE WITH COUSCOUS

In Morocco, this unusual tagine is prepared with conger eel.

INGREDIENTS 1.1 kg (2 lb 2 oz) sea bass with head, gutted and scaled │ 1½ teaspoons salt │ 1 small onion, studded with 2 cloves │ 5 stems of parsley with leaves │ 3 stems of coriander with leaves │ 1 large cinnamon stick │ 2 bay leaves │ 1.8 litres (3 pints) water │ 1¾ tablespoons extra virgin olive oil │ good pinch of saffron threads │ ¼–½ teaspoon black pepper │ ½ teaspoon turmeric │ 500 g (1 lb) red onions, sliced │ 2 garlic cloves │ 50 g (2 oz) raisins │ 50 g (2 oz) gold and green sultanas │ ¼ teaspoon ground cinnamon │ good pinch of freshly grated root ginger │ ½ tablespoon dark honey

COUSCOUS 375 g (12 oz) fine organic couscous │ 1 teaspoon salt │ 1 tablespoon extra virgin olive oil

ONE Rinse the fish, pat dry and sprinkle inside and out with ½ teaspoon of the salt. Cut off the head and trim the tail. Slice the fish into 3 pieces. Put the clove-studded onion, parsley, coriander, cinnamon stick and bay leaves in a pan and place the head and fish pieces on top. Add the water and bring slowly to the boil, skimming as foam forms. Add ¼ tablespoon oil and the saffron. Reduce the heat and simmer gently for 5 minutes. **TWO** Remove the fish, but leave the head and simmer for 40–50 minutes. Add the pepper and turmeric and cook for 10 minutes. **THREE** Meanwhile, gently sauté the onions in the remaining oil until translucent. Stir in the garlic and cook briefly, then add 300 ml (½ pint) of the stock. Simmer gently for 15 minutes. Add the dried fruit and cook until the onions are soft. Add the cinnamon, ginger and honey, increase the heat and simmer until the onions are caramelized. **FOUR** Meanwhile, cover the couscous with water, rake it through with your fingers, then drain and spread it over a large tray. Rake the grains with your fingers a few times to aerate them, then leave for 20–30 minutes until the water is absorbed and the couscous is relatively dry. Sprinkle with the salt and rub the grains between your palms to free them of any lumps. Place in the top of a couscoussière over boiling water (or in a sieve) and steam for 15 minutes. Transfer to a dish, sprinkle with the oil and mix gently to break up any lumps. Add about 300 ml (½ pint) of the stock and stir to combine. **FIVE** Serve the couscous topped with the fish and onions.

Serves 4–6

NUTRIENT ANALYSIS PER SERVING 2527 kJ – 600 kcal – 42 g protein – 83 g carbohydrate – 32 g sugars – 14 g fat – 2 g saturates – 4 g fibre – 1.3 g sodium

recipe illustrated on pages 176–177

VEGETABLES

MALLOW, AROMATIC HERBS AND OLIVES

Mallow is a plant that grows in the Mediterranean and the Middle East, and in many other parts of the world. In Morocco it is known as *Bekkoula*, in Lebanon as *Khobeiza* and in France as *Mauve*. The leaves contain a gelatinous substance that are anti-bacterial and anti-inflammatory. My grandmother treated skin conditions by wrapping them with mallow leaves, which were left until the condition cleared. She even boiled the leaves with water, to be drunk when a sore throat occurred or for any other inflammatory ailments. If mallow is not available, use spinach. Eat with barbecued chicken or fish.

INGREDIENTS 500 g (1 lb) mallow leaves or spinach | about 175 g (6 oz) parsley | about 150 g (5 oz) coriander stems with leaves | 3 garlic cloves, unpeeled | 125 g (4 oz) celery leaves, finely chopped | 1 teaspoon salt, or to taste | 2 tablespoons extra virgin olive oil | 4 tablespoons lemon juice | juice of 1 small orange | 1 teaspoon paprika | a few small slices of preserved lemon *(see page 17)* or fresh lemon | 10–12 halved violet or black olives, rinsed well | pinch of cayenne pepper, or to taste | pomegranate seeds or 1 tablespoon pomegranate syrup (optional) | black pepper

ONE Gather the mallow or spinach leaves in a bunch and slice finely, including any tender stems. Discard the parsley and coriander stems, gather the leaves in a bunch and chop finely. **TWO** Place the mallow or spinach and garlic in a pan over a very low heat and the remaining ingredients in a salad bowl. **THREE** When the greens have reduced in size, turn off the heat and remove the garlic. Discard the skin, then cream the garlic and add to the ingredients in the bowl. Leave the mallow mixture to cool for 5 minutes, then add to the bowl and toss. Taste and adjust the seasonings.

VARIATION: Steam the mallow, garlic and celery. When ready, cream the garlic and cool the mallow and celery. Add the parsley and coriander and toss with the remaining ingredients.

Serves 4–6

NUTRIENT ANALYSIS PER SERVING 533 kJ – 129 kcal – 6 g protein – 6 g carbohydrate – 5 g sugars – 9 g fat – 1 g saturates – 10 g fibre – 1 g sodium (if using 1 teaspoon salt)

HEALTHY TIP This dish is a blood purifier that lowers bad cholesterol (LDL). It contains a good amount of C and E vitamins, both powerful antioxidants to neutralize free radicals in the body. It is also rich in iron, magnesium, calcium and phosphorus.

recipe illustrated on pages 184–185

PEPPERS WITH TOMATOES

Here is one of the many delicious Moroccan starters of cooked vegetables. It's simple to make and marries well with meat, chicken and fish dishes. For vegetarians, eat with couscous or quinoa, which is rich in protein. For those who don't like hot chilli, use a mild one instead.

INGREDIENTS 3 green peppers | 1 chilli | 750 g (1½ lb) tomatoes | 1½–2 tablespoons extra virgin olive oil | ½–1 teaspoon paprika | 1 large garlic clove, crushed | 1 teaspoon tomato purée (optional) | 1 teaspoon salt, or to taste | 3 heaped tablespoons finely chopped coriander leaves | 2 heaped tablespoons finely chopped parsley | pinch of black pepper (optional)

ONE Place the green peppers and chilli on a heat diffuser over a medium gas flame. Turn them for 3–5 minutes to char all over – the chilli needs much less time, so keep an eye on it. Alternatively, preheat the grill to high, then grill the peppers for 18 minutes or until charred on all sides. **TWO** Meanwhile, skin, deseed and finely cube the tomatoes. Heat a medium–large shallow pan, add 1 tablespoon of the oil, the paprika, garlic, tomato purée, if using, and tomatoes and sprinkle with the salt. Give them a good stir and cook for 20 minutes or until the water has evaporated (some tomatoes have more water than others). **THREE** When the peppers and chilli are cool enough to handle, skin and deseed them, then cut into cubes. Add to the tomatoes with the coriander and parsley, stir in the remaining oil and cook for about a further 5 minutes. Sprinkle with the pepper, if using, and serve warm or at room temperature.

Serves 4–6

NUTRIENT ANALYSIS PER SERVING 454 kJ – 109 kcal – 4 g protein – 8 g carbohydrate – 7 g sugars – 7 g fat – 1 g saturates – 9 g fibre – 0.5 g sodium (if using 1 teaspoon salt)

HEALTHY TIP A dish with valuable amounts of E and C vitamins and the potent antioxidant lycopene, which may prevent prostate cancer. Chillies have long been used in pharmaceutical preparations and creams are made from them to calm and relieve rheumatism and arthritis. They help the circulation and are anti-cancerous and antiseptic.

recipe illustrated on pages 188–189

PULSES, GRAINS AND BARLEY COUSCOUS

A complex carbohydrate dish called *Urkimen*.

INGREDIENTS 75 g (3 oz) dried chickpeas, soaked overnight ⎪ 75 g (3 oz) dried broad beans, soaked overnight ⎪ 50 g (2 oz) dried corn or maize, soaked overnight ⎪ 1.8–2 litres (3–3½ pints) water ⎪ 65 g (2½ oz) dried haricot beans, soaked for 6 hours ⎪ 75 g (3 oz) brown lentils ⎪ 50 g (2 oz) dried peas ⎪ 500 g (1 lb) onions, sliced ⎪ 65 g (2½ oz) coarse bulgar wheat ⎪ 2 large tomatoes, skinned and diced ⎪ 1 medium aubergine, cut into chunks ⎪ 250 g (8 oz) carrots, cut into thick sticks ⎪ 1 large turnip, cut into thick sticks ⎪ 2½ tablespoons extra virgin olive oil ⎪ 2 courgettes, cubed ⎪ 2½ teaspoons paprika ⎪ ½–¾ teaspoon black pepper ⎪ 500 g (1 lb) barley semolina couscous (*belboula*) ⎪ salt

ONE Put the drained, rinsed chickpeas, broad beans and corn in a couscoussière, or pan, with the water. Bring slowly to the boil, skimming the surface. Cover and simmer for 1 hour. **TWO** Meanwhile, add the drained, rinsed haricot beans, lentils and peas to the pan. Skim again and add the onions. Bring to the boil, then simmer for 5–10 minutes. Add the bulgar, tomatoes and aubergine and simmer for 5–10 minutes. **THREE** Add the carrots, turnip and 1½ tablespoons oil and cook for 10 minutes. Add the courgettes and hot water if necessary and simmer for 5–10 minutes. Sprinkle with salt to taste, paprika and pepper. **FOUR** Cover the couscous with water. Rake it through with your fingers, then drain and spread it over a large tray. Rake the grains with your fingers to aerate, then leave for 20–30 minutes until the water is absorbed and they are dry. Rub the couscous gently between your palms to break up any lumps. Place in the top of the couscoussière, or sieve, over the grains and pulses and steam for 30 minutes, separating the grains twice with a fork. **FIVE** Remove and spread over a large tray, sprinkle with water and 1 teaspoon salt. Aerate and separate as before. Leave until the water is absorbed, then sprinkle with 1½ teaspoons salt and gently rub the grains. Steam for 30 minutes. **SIX** Remove and spread over a large tray, sprinkle with the remaining oil and a ladleful of stock, then mix, separate the grains and leave to absorb the water. Rub and steam again for 15 minutes, then serve with the grains and pulses.

Serves 8

NUTRIENT ANALYSIS PER SERVING 1645 kJ – 392 kcal – 16 g protein – 70 g carbohydrate – 9 g sugars – 6 g fat – 1 g saturates – 7 g fibre – 0.6 g sodium (if using 2½ teaspoons salt)

recipe illustrated on pages 192–193

AUBERGINE & PEPPER RATATOUILLE

In this Moroccan dish I don't use water and I cook the vegetables for a short period of time to preserve their nutrients. The tomatoes are skinned to be in harmony with the texture of the other vegetables, but you can keep their skins on, if preferred, which helps to retain more of their soluble vitamins. The dish has a good balance of acidic and non-acidic ingredients. When barbecuing, prepare it in advance to serve with meat, fish or chicken. Eat warm or at room temperature.

INGREDIENTS 2 large green or red peppers, or a mixture │ 500 g (1 lb) aubergines, cut into small cubes │ 300 g (10 oz) courgettes, cut into small cubes │ 625 g (1¼ lb) tomatoes, skinned, deseeded and cut into small cubes │ 2 large garlic cloves, crushed │ 1¼ teaspoons salt, or to taste │ 1 teaspoon paprika │ pinch of black pepper │ 2 whole chillies │ 1–2 tablespoons extra virgin olive or groundnut oil │ pinch of ground cumin (optional)

ONE Preheat the grill to high, then grill the peppers for 18 minutes or until charred on all sides. Alternatively, place the peppers on a heat diffuser over a medium gas flame. Turn them for 3–5 minutes to char all over. Leave the peppers to cool, then skin, deseed and cut the flesh into small cubes. Put to one side. **TWO** Put the aubergines, courgettes and tomatoes in a medium pan, stir in the garlic and sprinkle with the salt, paprika and pepper. Add the chillies and drizzle with the oil, then stir gently to help the vegetables release their liquid. Cover, place over a medium heat and simmer for 20 minutes, stirring gently 2–3 times during the cooking. **THREE** Stir in the pepper cubes and cook for 1–2 minutes, then sprinkle with the cumin, if using. Serve warm or cold.

Serves 4–5

NUTRIENT ANALYSIS PER SERVING 585 kJ – 139 kcal – 5 g protein – 15 g carbohydrate – 10 g sugars – 7 g fat – 1 g saturates – 6 g fibre – 0.6 g sodium (if using 1¼ teaspoons salt)

HEALTHY TIP Vegetables are indispensable for good health and are said to be anti-ageing. They are low in fat, have a high water content and are rich in fibre, important for good bowel function. When cooked, their fibre becomes easier to digest.

recipe illustrated on pages 196–197

MARINATED AUBERGINES

This tasty Moroccan preparation – called *Aubergines m'Rekked* – is quick to make and ideal to offer with a drink when friends are around.

INGREDIENTS 500 g (1 lb) baby aubergines | 5 garlic cloves | 3 tablespoons lemon juice | ¾ teaspoon ground cumin | 2–3 tablespoons finely chopped parsley | ¾ teaspoon sea salt | 1 teaspoon paprika | 1½ teaspoons ground coriander | 2 tablespoons extra virgin olive oil

ONE Steam the aubergines and garlic for 6–8 minutes until slightly soft. Place in a sieve and leave to drain well, then cut the aubergines lengthways into quarters to within 1 cm (½ inch) of the stem, leaving them attached at the end. **TWO** Peel the garlic, cream using a pestle and mortar and mix thoroughly with the remaining ingredients. **THREE** Gently push some of this mixture into each aubergine. Put the stuffed aubergines in a clean jar, cover tightly and leave for a few hours, then turn upside down. The aubergines will be ready to eat within 6 hours, but the flavours will slowly develop after 1–2 days.

Serves 6–8

NUTRIENT ANALYSIS PER SERVING 206 kJ – 50 kcal – 1 g protein – 2 g carbohydrate – 2 g sugars – 4 g fat – 1 g saturates – 2 g fibre – 0.3 g sodium

HEALTHY TIP These marinated aubergines act as a diuretic and may lower bad cholesterol.

AUBERGINE AND POTATO CAKES

Aubergines were introduced to Morocco by the Arabs. This magical vegetable enhances the flavour of whatever ingredient it is cooked with. The recipe in the book of Ibn Razine al-Tujibi, which is believed to have been written between 1238 and 1266, uses aubergine with minced lamb, but instead of lamb I opted for potatoes. Besides being nutritious, they are comforting and marry well with the aubergines. These cakes are delicious and crisp on the outside while remaining soft on the inside – children will like them and they are suitable for vegetarians and all ages. You can also make miniature ones to serve at parties.

INGREDIENTS 500 g (1 lb) aubergines, thickly sliced │ 4 garlic cloves, unpeeled │ 425 g (14 oz) potatoes, scrubbed and left whole │ 100 g (3½ oz) onion, grated │ 4 tablespoons finely chopped coriander leaves │ ¾ teaspoon salt │ ½ teaspoon ground cumin, or to taste │ pinch of paprika │ 1 egg white │ groundnut oil, for oiling and frying

ONE Steam the aubergines and garlic for 6–8 minutes. Remove the garlic and peel, then mash with the aubergines. **TWO** Steam the potatoes until cooked yet firm. Allow to cool, then grate coarsely and mix with the aubergines, onion, coriander, salt, cumin and paprika. Beat the egg white, then fold into the aubergine and potato mixture and leave for 5 minutes. Alternatively, to make shaping the cakes easier, put the mixture in the refrigerator for 5–10 minutes. **THREE** Oil your hands, then take a portion of the mixture and form into a 3 cm (1¼ inch) round. Heat the oil in a frying pan until hot, then fry the cakes until golden all over. Alternatively, grill for 3–5 minutes on each side until lightly browned, although they won't be as crisp. Drain on double kitchen paper and eat hot or at room temperature. Serve with Orange and Olive Salad *(see page 75)*.

Makes 14–16

NUTRIENT ANALYSIS PER SERVING 166 kJ – 39 kcal – 1 g protein – 7 g carbohydrate – 1 g sugars – 1 g fat – 0 g saturates – 1 g fibre – 0.1 g sodium

recipe illustrated on pages 202–203

CAULIFLOWER WITH SPICES

INGREDIENTS 1 tablespoon extra virgin olive oil | ¾ teaspoon ground coriander | 2 tablespoons coriander leaves, finely chopped | 200 g (7 oz) onions, sliced | 1.25 kg (2½ lb) cauliflower, broken into florets | a little under 150 ml (¼ pint) water, or as necessary | 2 teaspoons unbleached organic flour | good pinch of freshly grated root ginger | ¼ teaspoon ground cumin | 2–3 tablespoons lemon juice

ONE Heat the oil in a medium pan. Add the ground and fresh coriander, onions and cauliflower, stir well and add the water. Bring to the boil, then reduce the heat to very low, cover and simmer for 15–20 minutes. **TWO** Stir 1½ tablespoons of the cauliflower stock into the flour until smooth, then add to the cauliflower in the pan. Simmer for a few minutes, then season with ginger, cumin and lemon juice. Leave for 1–2 minutes for the flavours to develop, then serve warm or at room temperature.

VARIATION: The cauliflower florets can be steamed and then added to the other ingredients except the flour and water and be used as a salad. Taste and add more oil if necessary.

Serves 4–6

NUTRIENT ANALYSIS PER SERVING 680 kJ – 163 kcal – 12 g protein – 17 g carbohydrate – 11 g sugars – 6 g fat – 1 g saturates – 7 g fibre – 0.3 g sodium

AUBERGINE AND TOMATOES

This simple and healthy salad is known as *Zaalouk* in Morocco.

INGREDIENTS 500 g (1 lb) aubergines, sliced into medium pieces │ 3 garlic cloves, unpeeled │ ½ tablespoon lemon juice │ 250 g (8 oz) tomatoes, skinned, deseeded and cubed │ 2 tablespoons extra virgin olive oil │ 1 teaspoon salt, or to taste │ ½ teaspoon paprika │ ¾ teaspoon ground cumin │ 2 tablespoons finely chopped coriander leaves

ONE Steam the aubergines and garlic. When the aubergines are soft, transfer to a large dish. Peel the garlic, add to the aubergines with the lemon juice and mash together. **TWO** Put the tomatoes and 1 tablespoon of the oil in a medium frying pan. Sprinkle with the salt and simmer over a medium-low heat, stirring occasionally. **THREE** When nearly all the water has evaporated, stir in the aubergines, paprika, cumin, coriander and remaining oil. Stir well for 1–2 minutes, taste and adjust the seasonings and serve warm or at room temperature.

Serves 4

NUTRIENT ANALYSIS PER SERVING 339 kJ – 80 kcal – 2 g protein – 5 g carbohydrate – 4 g sugars – 6 g fat – 1 g saturates – 4 g fibre – 0.5 g sodium

COUSCOUS WITH MILK AND WALNUTS

INGREDIENTS 300 g (10 oz) organic couscous | ½ teaspoon salt | 75–125 g (3–4 oz) walnuts, finely ground | 1 teaspoon turmeric | ¼ teaspoon ground cinnamon | small pinch of dried lavender (optional) | 250 ml (8 fl oz) semi-skimmed milk | 1 bay leaf | 1 cinnamon stick | ½ tablespoon dark honey | 4–5 medjool dates, cubed

ONE Cover the couscous with water. Rake it through with your fingers, then drain and immediately spread it evenly over a large tray. Rake the grains with your fingers to aerate them, then leave for 20–30 minutes until the water is absorbed and the couscous is relatively dry. **TWO** When dry, rub the couscous gently between your palms to break down any lumps. Sprinkle the couscous with the salt, walnuts, turmeric, cinnamon and lavender, if using, and mix thoroughly. **THREE** Put the milk, bay leaf and cinnamon stick in a large pan and bring to the boil. Add the honey and stir until dissolved. Remove the bay leaf and cinnamon stick and take off the heat. **FOUR** Add the couscous to the hot milk, stir, cover and leave until the milk has been absorbed. Mix in the dates and serve warm.

Serves 4

NUTRIENT ANALYSIS PER SERVING 1723 kJ – 423 kcal – 10 g protein – 53 g carbohydrate – 14 g sugars – 19 g fat – 2 g saturates – 2 g fibre – 0.3 g sodium

COUSCOUS WITH SEVEN VEGETABLES

This is the national dish of Morocco.

INGREDIENTS 125 g (4 oz) dried chickpeas, soaked overnight │ 500 g (1 lb) boned lamb (leg or shoulder) │ 1.8 litres (3 pints) water │ 2 bay leaves │ 2 cinnamon sticks │ 5 small onions, about 500 g (1 lb), halved, each half cut into 3 │ good pinch of saffron threads │ 1 teaspoon ground ginger │ 1½ tablespoons extra virgin olive oil │ 3–4 coriander sprigs │ 3–4 parsley sprigs │ ½ small white cabbage, cut into 3 pieces │ 4 small carrots │ 1 turnip, quartered │ 1 aubergine, about 250 g (8 oz) │ 4 medium pieces of pumpkin, peeled and deseeded │ 4 baby courgettes │ 3 tomatoes, halved │ 2½ teaspoons salt, or to taste │ ¾ teaspoon black pepper │ good pinch of turmeric │ ¾–1 teaspoon paprika │ 375 g (12 oz) organic couscous

ONE Put the drained, rinsed chickpeas in a couscoussière, or pan, with the lamb, water, bay leaves and cinnamon. Bring slowly to the boil, skimming the surface. Cover and simmer for 5 minutes, then reduce the heat to low and simmer for 40 minutes. **TWO** Add the onions, saffron, ½ teaspoon ginger, ½ tablespoon oil, coriander and parsley, cover and cook for 15 minutes. Add the cabbage, carrots and turnip and cook for 10 minutes. **THREE** Cut the aubergine lengthways into quarters to within 1 cm (½ inch) of the stem, leaving it attached at the end. Add to the pan with the pumpkin, courgettes and tomatoes. Add 1¼ teaspoons salt, the remaining ginger, pepper, turmeric and paprika. Simmer for 10–15 minutes or until the meat and vegetables are tender. **FOUR** Cover the couscous with water. Rake it with your fingers, then drain and spread it over a large tray. Rake the grains with your fingers to aerate them, then leave for 20–30 minutes until the water is absorbed and the couscous is relatively dry. **FIVE** Rub gently between your palms, letting it fall back into the tray, to break down any lumps. Steam in the top of the couscoussière, or sieve, for 20–30 minutes. **SIX** Spread over a large tray, sprinkle with water and the remaining salt and aerate and separate the grains as before. Leave until the water is fully absorbed and gently rub again. Steam for 20–30 minutes. **SEVEN** Spread over a large tray, sprinkle with the remaining oil and 1–2 ladles stock and stir with a fork. **EIGHT** Serve topped with the vegetables and meat.

Serves 4–6

NUTRIENT ANALYSIS PER SERVING 2834 kJ – 676 kcal – 44 g protein – 90 g carbohydrate – 23 g sugars – 18 g fat – 6 g saturates – 13 g fibre – 1.1 g sodium (if using 2 teaspoons salt)

recipe illustrated on pages 210–211

PASTRIES

BRIOUATS WITH VEGETABLES

In Morocco, briouats, as a general rule, are served as starters along with the salads. They're invariably filled and are packed with good nutrients. Here, they are filled with a mixture of colourful vegetables – the pastry disguise might attract children to eat some. They are excellent to serve at parties, since they can be prepared ahead of time.

INGREDIENTS 1 tablespoon extra virgin olive oil │ 1 teaspoon clarified butter *(see page 18)* │ 200 g (7 oz) turnip, coarsely grated │ 200 g (7 oz) carrots, coarsely grated │ 200 g (7 oz) courgettes, coarsely grated │ 1 teaspoon salt │ ½ teaspoon turmeric (optional) │ 1 teaspoon black pepper │ 4 sheets of filo pastry, or as necessary │ 1 egg yolk, beaten │ groundnut oil, for brushing │ chopped mint, to garnish

ONE Heat a frying pan, add the oil and butter and heat until melted. Add the vegetables and cook for 8 minutes or until they reduce in size. Season with the salt, turmeric, if using, and pepper. Remove from the heat and leave to cool. **TWO** Meanwhile, fold the filo sheets in half and, using scissors, cut strips of 6 cm (2½ inch) widths. Keep those not in use under a wet cloth. Take 1 heaped teaspoon of the vegetable mixture and place in the corner at the narrow end of one filo strip. Fold this corner up and over on the diagonal to make a triangle shape, then keep folding, left then right, until there is just one fold to go. Moisten the end of the filo with beaten egg yolk, make the last fold and gently press on the triangle to seal. Repeat with the remaining filling and filo. **THREE** Brush lightly all over with oil, place on a baking sheet and bake in a preheated oven, 180°C (350°F) Gas Mark 4, for 15 minutes or until golden in colour. Serve with a sprinkling of chopped mint leaves.

Makes 16–18

NUTRIENT ANALYSIS PER SERVING 1214 kJ – 50 kcal – 1 g protein – 7 g carbohydrate – 2 g sugars – 2 g fat – 1 g saturates – 1 g fibre – 0.2 g sodium

HEALTHY TIP These briouats are nutritious, rich in betacarotene, potassium, niacin and calcium. They contain little saturated fat.

recipe illustrated on pages 218–219

BRIOUATS WITH GOATS' CHEESE

These briouats enclose a mixture of goats' cheese and parsley, and would be good to serve at any occasion, even at a picnic. Briouats are made with many interesting fillings, so experiment with your own ideas. For instance, for this recipe try adding some pitted and chopped black olives, and use mint instead of parsley.

INGREDIENTS 150 g (5 oz) soft goats' cheese │ 4 heaped tablespoons finely chopped parsley │ pinch of black pepper │ pinch of salt, if necessary │ 2 sheets of filo pastry, or as necessary │ 1 egg yolk, beaten │ groundnut oil, for brushing

ONE Mix the cheese, parsley and pepper together thoroughly. Taste the cheese mixture and if necessary add the salt. **TWO** Slice the filo sheets into strips of 6 cm (2½ inch) widths. Keep those not in use under a wet cloth. Take 1 tablespoon of the cheese mixture and place in the corner at the narrow end of one filo strip. Fold this corner up and over on the diagonal to make a triangle shape, then keep folding, left then right, until there is just one fold to go. Moisten the end of the filo with beaten egg yolk, make the last fold and gently press on the triangle to seal. Repeat with the remaining filling and filo. **THREE** Brush lightly all over with oil, place on a baking sheet and bake in a preheated oven, 180°C (350°F) Gas Mark 4, for 15 minutes or until deep golden in colour.

Makes 14

NUTRIENT ANALYSIS PER SERVING 188 kJ – 45 kcal – 2 g protein – 3 g carbohydrate – 0 g sugars – 3 g fat – 1 g saturates – 0 g fibre – 0.07 g sodium

BRIOUATS WITH PRAWNS AND SEA BASS

For non-lovers of fish, this may be an excellent way to include it in the diet. The prawns and sea bass are steamed for a short time, and then combined with olive oil, lemon juice, coriander and cumin. Briouats are very versatile as they can be filled with any fish, such as monkfish, langoustines, salmon or tuna, or with meat, fruit or nuts.

INGREDIENTS 600 ml (1 pint) water | 1 parsley sprig | 1 slice of lemon | 1 bay leaf | 12 large raw prawns, peeled | 300 g (10 oz) sea bass fillets | 1–1½ tablespoons extra virgin olive oil | ¾ teaspoon ground cumin | handful of finely chopped coriander leaves | 3 tablespoons lemon juice, or to taste | 1 teaspoon salt | about ¼ teaspoon black pepper | 3 sheets of filo pastry, or as necessary | 1 egg yolk, beaten | groundnut oil, for brushing

ONE Put the water, parsley, lemon and bay leaf in the bottom half of a couscoussière, or pan, and bring to the boil. Put the prawns and sea bass into the perforated top section, or a steamer, and steam for 3–4 minutes, then remove and leave to cool. Chop the prawns and fish into medium-sized pieces. **TWO** Heat the oil in a frying pan, then add the chopped prawns and fish, the cumin and coriander and cook, stirring, for a few seconds. Add the lemon juice, salt and pepper, remove from the heat and leave to cool. **THREE** Fold the filo sheets in half and, using scissors, cut strips of 6 cm (2½ inch) widths. Keep those not in use under a wet cloth. Take 1 heaped teaspoon of the fish mixture and place in the corner at the narrow end of one filo strip. Fold this corner up and over on the diagonal to make a triangle shape, then keep folding, left then right, until there is just one fold to go. Moisten the end of the filo with beaten egg yolk, make the last fold and gently press on the triangle to seal. Repeat with the remaining filling and filo. **FOUR** Brush lightly all over with oil, place on a baking sheet and bake in a preheated oven, 180°C (350°F) Gas Mark 4, for 15 minutes or until deep golden in colour.

Makes about 21

NUTRIENT ANALYSIS PER SERVING 198 kJ – 47 kcal – 4 g protein – 3 g carbohydrate – 0 g sugars – 2 g fat – 0 g saturates – 0 g fibre – 0.2 g sodium

HEALTHY TIP These briouats are very nutritious, supplying zinc, vitamin E and omega-3 oils, which are important for the normal function of the immune system and more so for men who lose zinc. Olive oil is rich in vitamin E.

recipe illustrated on pages 224–225

BRIOUATS WITH MEAT

These irresistible triangles are to die for – as you bite into one, you will want to have more and more. Briouats are easy to make, and freeze well, to be reheated when needed.

INGREDIENTS 1 tablespoon extra virgin olive oil │ 150 g (5 oz) onions, finely chopped │ 1 red pepper, about 150 g (5 oz), cored, deseeded and finely chopped │ 1 green pepper, about 150 g (5 oz), cored, deseeded and finely chopped │ 1 teaspoon ground cumin │ ¾ teaspoon paprika │ ¼ teaspoon black pepper │ 250 g (8 oz) minced lamb │ ¾ teaspoon salt │ 3 heaped tablespoons finely chopped coriander leaves │ 3 heaped tablespoons finely chopped parsley │ 5 sheets of filo pastry, or as necessary │ 1 egg yolk, beaten │ groundnut oil, for brushing

ONE Heat a fairly large frying pan. Add the oil, onions and chopped peppers and cook, stirring occasionally, for 3–5 minutes. Season with the cumin, paprika and pepper and stir well, then add the lamb and salt and cook the meat for 3–4 minutes, stirring, to brown thoroughly. Continue to cook, stirring occasionally, until any liquid has almost evaporated but it has not dried out. Just before the end of cooking time, stir in the coriander and parsley. **TWO** Fold the filo sheets in half and, using scissors, cut strips of 6 cm (2½ inch) widths. Keep those not in use under a wet cloth. Take 1 heaped teaspoon of the meat mixture and place in the corner at the narrow end of one filo strip. Fold this corner up and over on the diagonal to make a triangle shape, then keep folding, left then right, until there is just one fold to go. Moisten the end of the filo with beaten egg yolk, make the last fold and gently press on the triangle to seal. Repeat with the remaining filling and filo. **THREE** Brush lightly all over with oil, place on a baking sheet and bake in a preheated oven, 180°C (350°F) Gas Mark 4, for 15–20 minutes or until golden in colour.

Makes 24

NUTRIENT ANALYSIS PER SERVING 220 kJ – 53 kcal – 3 g protein – 5 g carbohydrate – 1 g sugars – 2 g fat – 1 g saturates – 0 g fibre – 0.2 g sodium

HEALTHY TIP These are rich in protein, betacarotene, vitamin C, phosphorus, magnesium and iron.

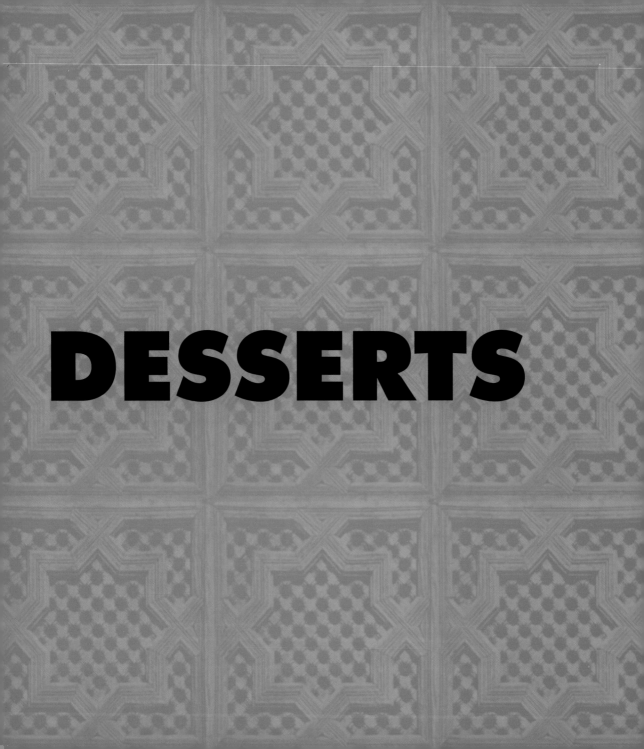

DESSERTS

ORANGE CONFITURE

You can't visit Marrakech or any other city in Morocco and not be tempted to prepare an orange or clementine confiture, since the fruits are cultivated there and you see them everywhere. So when oranges are in season, at their juiciest and have a beautiful orange colour, prepare this confiture. This is delicious on its own, with Rice Milk Pudding *(see page 241)*, Rice Pudding with Almonds *(see page 236)*, in a fruit salad or as a filling for a sponge cake. Use within 2–3 weeks.

INGREDIENTS 1 kg (2 lb) navel oranges, scrubbed │ 275 g (9 oz) fructose (fruit sugar) │ 300 ml (½ pint) water │ 2 teaspoons lemon juice │ 2–3 cloves

ONE Bring a large pan of water to the boil, add the oranges and boil rapidly for 1 minute. Using a slotted spoon, transfer the oranges to a bowl of iced water and leave for 10 minutes. **TWO** Cut the oranges into 1 cm (½ inch) slices. Do not remove the seeds. Put the orange slices in a large shallow pan in a single layer. If necessary, cut a few slices in small pieces to fit in the gaps. Remove from the pan and put to one side. **THREE** Put 200 g (7 oz) of the fructose in the pan, cover with water and place over a low heat, shaking the pan until the sugar dissolves. Bring to the boil and add 1 teaspoon of the lemon juice and the cloves, then place the orange slices, and orange pieces if necessary, in the pan in a single layer. Return to the boil, then reduce the heat to medium-low and simmer for 10–15 minutes, until most of the water has evaporated. **FOUR** Sprinkle all over with the remaining fructose, shake the pan, increase the heat and leave to caramelize on one side, then turn to colour the other side. Turn the heat off. You should be left with about 2 tablespoons of the caramel sauce. **FIVE** Transfer the confiture to a bowl, cover with clingfilm and keep refrigerated for up to 3 weeks.

Makes about 1 kg (2 lb)

NUTRIENT ANALYSIS FOR TOTAL QUANTITY 5743 kJ – 1344 kcal – 8 g protein – 348 g carbohydrate – 348 g sugars – 1 g fat – 0 g saturates – 13 g fibre – 0.03 g sodium

GAZELLE'S HORNS

INGREDIENTS 75 g (3 oz) almonds, with skin on │ 125 g (4 oz) blanched almonds │ 1 teaspoon groundnut oil or clarified butter *(see page 18)*, plus oil for greasing │ 2 teaspoons orange flower water │ pinch of black pepper │ 2 teaspoons icing sugar │ 1 teaspoon dark honey │ pinch of ground cinnamon │ pinch of ground ginger │ small pinch of ground cloves │ 1 egg white │ 4 heaped tablespoons sesame seeds, or as necessary

ONE Put all the almonds in a food processor and whiz to a smooth consistency. Turn out into a bowl and add the oil or butter, flower water, pepper, icing sugar, honey, cinnamon, ginger and cloves and knead to mix thoroughly. If it's not malleable enough, add a little water. **TWO** Divide the mixture into 10 pieces, roll each piece into a small sausage and then into a crescent shape. **THREE** Beat the egg white and lightly brush a baking sheet with oil. Roll each crescent in the egg white, then in the sesame seeds and place on the baking sheet. Bake in a preheated oven, 180°C (350°F) Gas Mark 4, for 10–15 minutes or until browned. **FOUR** Remove from the oven and leave to cool.

Makes 10

NUTRIENT ANALYSIS PER SERVING 678 kJ – 164 kcal – 6 g protein – 3 g carbohydrate – 3 g sugars – 15 g fat – 1 g saturates – 3 g fibre – 0.01 g sodium

RICE PUDDING WITH ALMONDS

This is a succulent pudding and very easy to prepare. A similar one is prepared all over the Levant and Middle Eastern countries, and may be the origin of this pudding. It is said that the Crusaders fell for its exotic aroma, so they brought its recipe back to England in the 12th or 13th century. The original recipe calls for soaking the almonds in milk, then pressing them to extract the almond milk, while here the pulp is also used.

INGREDIENTS 75 g (3 oz) blanched almonds │ ½–1 teaspoon extra virgin olive oil │ ½ teaspoon icing sugar │ 75 g (3 oz) ground rice │ 600 ml (1 pint) semi-skimmed milk │ 65 g (2½ oz) fructose (fruit sugar) │ ¼–½ teaspoon mastic (gum arabic), ground with a little icing sugar, or a little vanilla extract │ 1–1¼ tablespoons orange flower water

ONE Whiz 50 g (2 oz) of the almonds in a food processor until smooth and powder-like. **TWO** Heat the oil in a small frying pan and sauté the remaining whole almonds over a low heat, stirring occasionally, until golden brown. Remove and sprinkle with icing sugar, then leave to cool and chop coarsely. **THREE** Put the rice and ground almonds in a pan and gradually whisk in the milk. Place the pan over a medium heat and bring to the boil, stirring continuously with a wooden spoon. Keep stirring and add the fructose. Once the sugar has dissolved, add the mastic or vanilla and the flower water and stir for 1–2 minutes or until it thickens. Pour into a serving dish and spread evenly, then leave to cool. **FOUR** Decorate all over with the reserved chopped almonds and chill before serving.

Serves 6–8

NUTRIENT ANALYSIS PER SERVING 909 kJ – 217 kcal – 7 g protein – 28 g carbohydrate – 17 g sugars – 9 g fat – 2 g saturates – 2 g fibre – 0.06 g sodium

HEALTHY TIP Rice pudding is healthy and light on the stomach. The milk and almonds ensure this is highly rich in calcium, an essential mineral to build strong bones and teeth and to maintain and reduce blood pressure.

recipe illustrated on pages 238–239

RICE MILK PUDDING

This recipe can also be served with a coulis of strawberries or mangoes.

INGREDIENTS 200 g (7 oz) white basmati rice, rinsed once and drained │ 600 ml (1 pint) water │ bouquet garni: 1 bay leaf, 1 cinnamon stick, 1 piece of fresh root ginger, 1 cardamom pod │ pinch of salt │ 600–750 ml (1–1¼ pints) semi-skimmed milk │ 1½–2 tablespoons fructose (fruit sugar) │ ¾–1 tablespoon orange flower water │ 5 g (¼ oz) butter

ONE Combine the rice, water, bouquet garni and salt in a medium pan. Bring to the boil, then reduce the heat to low, cover and simmer for 10–15 minutes or until the water has been absorbed and rice has softened but is still moist. **TWO** Remove the cinnamon stick. Add a little of the milk and stir every now and then until the rice absorbs the milk. Repeat until all the milk has been added and absorbed. Remove the ginger, cardamom and bay leaf. Stir in the fructose, flower water and butter. **THREE** Pour the milk and rice mixture into a blender or liquidizer and pulse briefly – it should be coarsely crushed, not puréed. Pour it back into the pan and heat for 2–3 minutes, stirring a few times. Transfer to a glass bowl and serve warm or chilled.

Serves 6–8

NUTRIENT ANALYSIS PER SERVING 777 kJ – 185 kcal – 6 g protein – 35 g carbohydrate – 9 g sugars – 2 g fat – 1 g saturates – 1 g fibre – 0.06 g sodium

HEALTHY TIP A soothing dish that's rich in protein, calcium, vitamin E, phosphorus, potassium and magnesium. Milk may control high blood pressure and reduce the risk of osteoporosis and this is a fabulous way to increase the consumption of milk – you'll see for yourself how enjoyable it is.

DRIED FRUIT SALAD

While in Fez I was told that the first fruit *b'steeya* was prepared by a woman who worked at the Royal Palace for King Hassan to honour Margaret Thatcher, England's then prime minister. Here, dried fruits are simmered in water with various aromatic spices. Once cooled, they can be added to a seasonal fresh fruit salad with some chopped mint.

INGREDIENTS 50 g (2 oz) dried apricots │ 75 g (3 oz) dried figs │ 65 g (2½ oz) prunes │ 40 g (1½ oz) raisins │ 25 g (1 oz) sun-dried apples │ 4–6 dried medjool dates │ bouquet garni: 1 cinnamon stick, 1 bay leaf, 2 cardamom pods, 1–2 cloves, 1 star anise │ 2 tablespoons fructose (fruit sugar) (optional) │ 1 teaspoon lemon juice │ pinch of nutmeg │ pinch of ground cinnamon │ good pinch of freshly grated root ginger │ 1 teaspoon orange flower water

ONE Rinse the dried fruits well, drain and place in a bowl. Cover with water and soak for 6 hours or overnight. **TWO** The following day, place the fruit and any remaining water in a pan with the bouquet garni and bring to the boil over a medium-low heat. You may need to add a little water. Simmer for 10 minutes, remove the bouquet garni and sprinkle with the fructose, if using, and the lemon juice, then simmer until the liquid has a slightly syrupy consistency. **THREE** Sprinkle with the nutmeg, cinnamon, ginger and flower water and give it a good stir. Remove from the heat and leave to cool. Serve as above.

Serves 6–8

NUTRIENT ANALYSIS PER SERVING 458 kJ – 107 kcal – 2 g protein – 26 g carbohydrate – 26 g sugars – 0 g fat – 0 g saturates – 6 g fibre – 0.02 g sodium (Note: analysis does not include optional fructose.)

HEALTHY TIP This fruit salad is very rich in betacarotene, E and B vitamins, iron and magnesium.

recipe illustrated on pages 244–245

BEGHRIR

These are crêpes, much loved by the Moroccans. They are eaten sprinkled with icing sugar or bathed in honey. When a mother gives birth, it is customary to serve her crêpes for breakfast. Unsurprisingly, they're high in energy and very tasty. Here I use wholemeal flour, which is superior to white flour and has valuable amounts of the B vitamins, important for the proper functioning of the body's nervous system. On Sundays, after my morning run, I take one of these crêpes out of my refrigerator, brush its smooth side lightly with butter and place under a hot grill for a few seconds to crisp. I eat it with a little good quality organic honey, a small piece of cheese and whatever fruit is available, be it banana, mango, strawberries, papaya or blueberries.

INGREDIENTS ½ teaspoon double-action yeast │ ¾ teaspoon sugar │ 75 g (3 oz) wholemeal flour │ 25 g (1 oz) plain flour │ 175 ml (6 fl oz) water │ 75 ml (3 fl oz) milk │ 1 egg │ ½ teaspoon whisky (optional) │ groundnut oil, for brushing

ONE Dissolve the yeast in a small cup with the sugar and 2 teaspoons of warm water, cover and leave in a warm place. **TWO** Sift the flours into a bowl, pushing as much bran as you can through the sieve, then tip any bran remaining in the sieve into the bowl. **THREE** Pour the water and milk into a small pan and heat to warm. Meanwhile, beat the egg and whisky, if using, in a small cup. Remove the milk mixture from the heat and, using a whisk, gradually whisk it into the flours with the yeast and the beaten egg mixture. Beat well to aerate the batter, then cover with a thick cloth and leave to rise in a warm place for 2 hours. **FOUR** Set a medium-small nonstick frying pan over a medium heat and brush lightly with oil. Whisk the batter again. When the pan is hot, pour a ladleful of the batter into the centre. It will run to form a round crêpe. Cook for 20–30 seconds, or until the surface is dry, shaking the pan slightly. Transfer to a warm plate and repeat with the remaining batter, stirring the batter in the bowl every now and then. Oil the pan after every 2–3 crêpes using an oil-dampened piece of kitchen paper. **FIVE** Serve hot with honey, or as described above.

Serves 8

NUTRIENT ANALYSIS PER SERVING 326 kJ – 78 kcal – 3 g protein – 9 g carbohydrate – 1 g sugars – 3 g fat – 1 g saturates – 1 g fibre – 0.02 g sodium (Note: analysis does not include optional whisky.)

HEALTHY TIP This is a meal in itself, containing a wealth of vitamins, minerals, antioxidants and protein, each of which has a role in maintaining a healthy mind and body, glowing skin and shining hair.

recipe illustrated on pages 248–249

GHORIBA

These biscuits are a little like shortbread – crunchy and smooth.

INGREDIENTS 2–3 tablespoons clarified butter, melted *(see page 18)* | 3 tablespoons groundnut oil | 150 g (5 oz) flour | 40 g (1½ oz) icing sugar | 1 tablespoon orange flower water | 1 tablespoon water | 2 cardamom pods, seeds finely crushed in ¼ teaspoon icing sugar | 40 g (1½ oz) coarsely chopped almonds

ONE Pour the butter and oil into a bowl, sift in the flour and stir in the icing sugar, flower water, water and ground cardamom. **TWO** Knead the mixture for 1–2 minutes in the bowl to bring it together, then turn out on to a clean surface. At first it may be crumbly, but keep kneading, shape it into a ball and put back in the bowl. Cover and leave to rest for about 30 minutes. **THREE** Remove the dough and knead again, then add the almonds and form into a ball as before. Pinch off a little dough the size of a walnut and roll and press between your palms to form a round. As you press it will naturally crack around its edges. Repeat with the remaining dough. **FOUR** Place the rounds on a baking sheet and cook in a preheated oven, 180°C (350°F) Gas Mark 4, for 10–15 minutes. The bases will brown and the tops will have a white cream colour. Remove the biscuits from the oven, leave to cool, then serve with a sprinkling of icing sugar.

Makes 10

NUTRIENT ANALYSIS PER SERVING 676 kJ – 160 kcal – 2 g protein – 16 g carbohydrate – 5 g sugars – 10 g fat – 4 g saturates – 1 g fibre – 0 g sodium

ACKNOWLEDGEMENTS

AUTHOR ACKNOWLEDGEMENTS This book wouldn't have been realized without the help and encouragement of many to whom I wish to express my immense gratitude and heartfelt thanks:

To Rosy Kindersley of Books for Cooks in London.

To my husband Nabil and my daughter Nour for her accurate remarks.

To my brother, Fouad Kanso.

To Professor Mohammed Mezzine and Laila Benkirane for their inspirational gift, the book they have translated from Arabic to French "Fudalat al-khiwan" fi Tayibat al-taâm wa al alwan.

To Professor Lahlou for his kindness, Abdelrafii Benjelloun chef lecturer, for his great help.

To Omar Lebrar of Dar el–Ghalia.

Many thanks to Marise Bergel for her precious time and effort.

To the National Tourism of Morocco.

To Aziz Murii for his time.

To Royal Maroc Airways.

To Ahmed Nait of Travelink who with devotion made my journey through Morocco most enjoyable.

To his equipe who guided me with great care: Siddik Assem, Said Lemri and Hisham in Fez.

My heartfelt thanks to Monsieur and Madame Sefraoui of the beautiful Riad Fez for their warmth and sharing the secrets of their delicious cooking.

Many thanks to Christope Robin, Jocelyne Leb and Fabrizio Ruspoli of La Maison Arabe in Marrakech for his time sharing his insight about Morocco, especially Tangier.

My immense thanks to Melle Boukraa F. in Rabat, and to the owners and staff of Loulema Essaouria, Kasbah Farm, Sawadi Skouraa, Kasbah Asma Rissani and El-minzah Hotel in Tangier – I still remember their lovely puff pastry Pastilla.

To my agent Deborah Rogers for having my best interests at.heart, and to Hannah Westland.

To Suzanne Walsh.

To Diane Klat.

To Nicola Hill for her devotion in making this book, Alice Bowden, William Reavell, Leigh Jones, Sunil Vijayaker, Liz Hippisley and to all who worked on it.

EXECUTIVE EDITOR Nicky Hill

EDITOR Charlotte Macey

DEPUTY CREATIVE DIRECTOR AND DESIGN Geoff Fennell

PHOTOGRAPHY William Reavell

FOOD STYLIST Sunil Vijayakar

PROP STYLIST Liz Hippisley

SENIOR PRODUCTION CONTROLLER Martin Croshaw

PICTURE ACKNOWLEDGEMENTS
All photography © Octopus Publishing Group Limited/ William Reavell with the exception of the following: Octopus Publishing Group Limited/Gus Filgate 19, 32, 50–1, 59, 123–3, 132–3, 136, 148, 150, 161, 186, 190, 196–7, 200, 248–9; Ian Alexander/Natural Patterns Website (http://easyweb.easynet.co.uk/ ~iany/index.htm) 3 background.